BIARRITZ TRAVEL GUIDE 2025

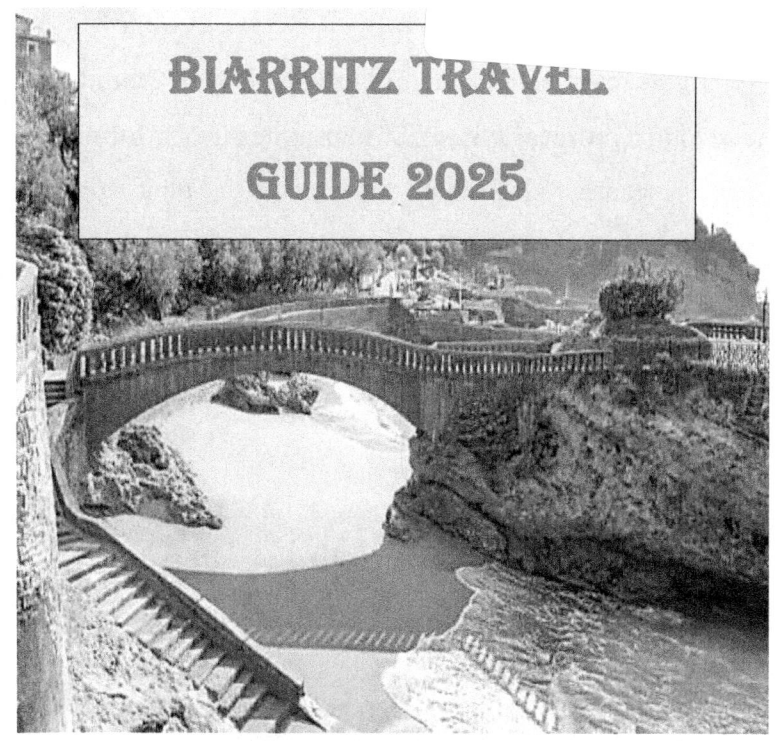

THE TRAVELER HANDBOOK FOR EXPLORING THE BASQUE CITY OF FRANCE

FRANCIS S. GEORGE

Copyright © 2024 by Francis S. George

All rights reserved. No part of this book may be reproduced, stored in a retrieval system, or transmitted in any form or by any means, electronic, mechanical, photocopying, recording, or otherwise, without the prior written permission of the publisher.

SCAN THE QR CODE BELOW TO GET ACCESS TO MORE BOOKS BY THE AUTHOR

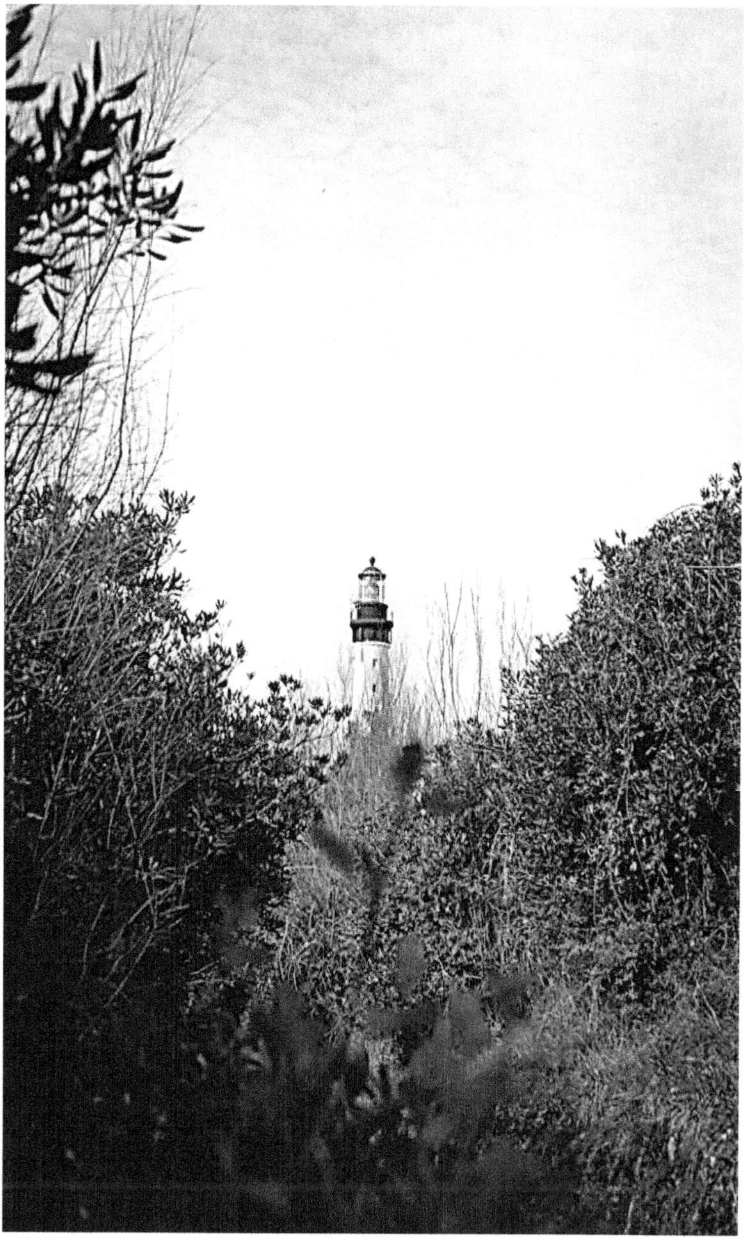

TABLE OF CONTENTS

INTRODUCTION TO BIARRITZ 7

CHAPTER 1 11

    OVERVIEW OF BIARRITZ 11
    THE BASQUE COUNTRY: HISTORY, TRADITIONS, AND
    LANGUAGE 12
    EXPLORING THE BASQUE ARCHITECTURE AND ART 15
    GEOGRAPHY AND CLIMATE 18
    FUN FACTS ABOUT BIARRITZ 21

CHAPTER 2 25

    GETTING TO AND NAVIGATING BIARRITZ 25
    AIRPORT INFORMATION 26
    TRAIN AND BUS SERVICES 30

CHAPTER 3 34

    ACCOMMODATIONS 34
    HOTELS AND RESORTS OF BIARRITZ 35
    UNIQUE BOUTIQUE STAYS AND VACATION RENTALS 39
    AIRBNB AND VACATION RENTALS 42
    CAMPING OPTIONS 45

CHAPTER 4 48

CULINARY DELIGHTS 48
BASQUE CUISINE 49
MUST-TRY DISHES AND LOCAL SPECIALTIES 52
RENOWNED RESTAURANTS AND CAFÉS 55
PINTXOS CRAWL 59
LOCAL MARKETS AND FOOD FESTIVALS 62

CHAPTER 5 66

TOP ATTRACTIONS AND SIGHTS 66
THE ICONIC BIARRITZ BEACH AND PROMENADE 67
THE ROCHER DE LA VIERGE 70
THE BIARRITZ LIGHTHOUSE 74
THE BIARRITZ CASINO 78
THE MUSÉE DE LA MER 81
THE COTE DES BASQUES 84
THE BIARRITZ AQUARIUM 88

CHAPTER 6 92

OUTDOOR ADVENTURES 92
SURFING AND WATER SPORTS IN BIARRITZ 93
HIKING AND EXPLORING THE STUNNING COASTLINE ... 96
CYCLING AND DISCOVERING THE SURROUNDING
COUNTRYSIDE 99
GOLF COURSES 102

4

CASINO BARRIÈRE 105

CHAPTER 7 110

DAY TRIPS FROM BIARRITZ 110
SAN SEBASTIÁN, SPAIN 111
BAYONNE AND ANGLET 114
PYRENEES MOUNTAINS 118

CHAPTER 8 124

PRACTICAL TIPS AND INFORMATION 124
VISA AND ENTRY REQUIREMENTS 125
LOCAL LAWS AND CUSTOMS 128
CURRENCY AND BUDGET PLANNING 131
SHOPPING AND SOUVENIRS 134
HEALTH AND SAFETY CONSIDERATIONS 137
SAFETY TIPS AND EMERGENCY CONTACTS 140

CONCLUSION 144

BIDDING FAREWELL TO BIARRITZ 145

6

INTRODUCTION TO BIARRITZ

Biarritz is a charming town that has been entrancing tourists for generations. The waves of the Atlantic Ocean have been caressing the craggy coastline of Biarritz for a very long time. The city of Biarritz, which is located in the Pyrenees Mountains and is surrounded by sparkling waters, has a history that is just as rich and captivating as the natural beauty that makes up its surroundings.

At the beginning of the 19th century, Biarritz was a peaceful fishing community inhabited by hardy Basque people who made a livelihood from the sea. On the other hand, life was about to take an unexpected turn for this seemingly unremarkable coastal town. Through the entrance of the French Empress Eugénie, wife of Napoleon III, in the year 1854, Biarritz would undergo a transformation that would last forever.

In the summer, the Empress chose to make Biarritz her summer hideaway because she was captivated by the town's gorgeous surroundings and pleasant temperature. As a result, she attracted the attention of Europe's elite. As soon as this newfound playground by the sea became available, lavish beachfront homes and great hotels began to spring up, catering to the affluent and aristocratic individuals who descended upon it.

As the town of Biarritz gained a reputation for being a fashionable resort town, its cultural prominence also increased accordingly. Artists and intellectuals were drawn to it because of the captivating combination of modern sophistication and Basque tradition that it possessed.

The picturesque streets and breathtaking coastline of Biarritz served as a source of creativity for several famous authors, including Victor Hugo, Edith Wharton, and Ernest Hemingway. Yet, Biarritz's past is not without its darker times. During the Spanish Civil War and World War II, this quaint town was at the center of complex geopolitical currents, bearing witness to the ebb and flow of conflict. Through it all, the resilience and spirit of the Basque people have endured, ensuring that Biarritz remains a captivating destination that seamlessly blends its rich past with a vibrant present.

Today, when you explore Biarritz's magnificent promenades and stare out at the pounding surf, you can't help but sense the weight of history that lingers in the air. From Empress Eugénie's opulent homes to the coastal baths that formerly serviced the wealthy, the past is ever-present, encouraging you to unearth the layers of this extraordinary town.

Within the pages of this travel book, you will go on a trip through Biarritz's enthralling history, discovering the sights, sounds, and tales that have made this Basque treasure a renowned destination for generations.

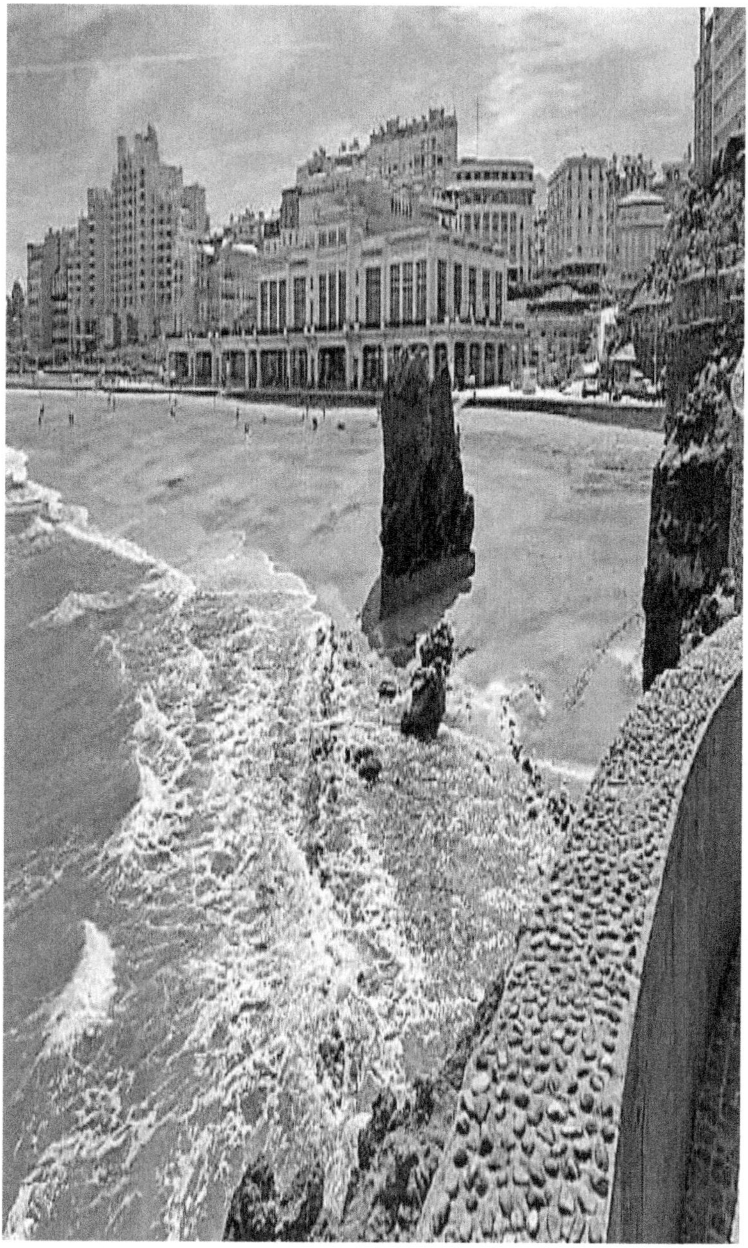

CHAPTER 1

OVERVIEW OF BIARRITZ

THE BASQUE COUNTRY: HISTORY, TRADITIONS, AND LANGUAGE

The Basque Country, a unique and enchanting territory that straddles the border between France and Spain, is a cultural wonder that has captured the hearts and minds of tourists and researchers alike. Within this large and varied territory sits the picturesque seaside town of Biarritz, France, which provides a rich tapestry of history, customs, and a unique language that sets it apart from the rest of the nation.

Biarritz's history may be traced back to the early 19th century when the coastal town was converted from a tiny fishing hamlet into a popular vacation destination. In the 1850s, the French Emperor Napoleon III and his wife, Empress Eugénie, discovered the attractions of Biarritz and helped to establish it as a favorite holiday location for the European elite. The town's exquisite architecture, magnificent beaches, and dynamic cultural life quickly drew a continuous stream of nobles, artists, and intellectuals, who came to Biarritz to enjoy its unique combination of refinement and natural beauty. As the town's fame expanded, Biarritz became a center for the Basque people, who had long occupied the territory on both sides of the border. The Basques, an old ethnic group with a rich cultural legacy, have a distinct language (Euskara) and customs that distinguish them apart from the rest of France and Spain. In Biarritz, the Basque influence can be observed in the town's architecture, gastronomy, and the exciting festivals and festivities that take place throughout the year.

The Basque people of Biarritz are recognized for their rich cultural traditions, which have been meticulously kept and handed down through centuries. One of the most prominent of these traditions is the yearly feast of Saint-Jean-Baptiste, or the Fête de la Saint-Jean, which takes place on June 24th. This historic holiday, which has its origins in pagan customs, is highlighted by bonfires, traditional dances, and the eating of Basque specialties such as the famed Bayonne ham and local wines.

Another strongly embedded institution in Biarritz is the sport of pelota, a handball-like game that is played on specific courts across the Basque Country. Pelota is more than simply a sport; it is a way of life for many Basques and is a source of immense pride and communal identity.

Spectators go to the pelota courts to see the intense, fast-paced contests, which are typically accompanied by traditional Basque music and the rhythmic chanting of the audience.

The Basque language, known as Euskara, is a unique and fascinating linguistic phenomenon that has enthralled scholars and language aficionados for centuries. Euskara is thought to be one of the oldest languages in Europe, having origins that may be traced back thousands of years. Unlike the Romance languages spoken in the surrounding areas, Euskara is not connected to any other known language, making it a linguistic isolate with a separate grammar, lexicon, and pronunciation.

Among Biarritz, the Basque language is still commonly spoken, notably among the elder generations. The town's citizens take great pride in their linguistic history and strive relentlessly to promote the use of Euskara in daily life, from the school to the marketplace. Visitors to Biarritz may immerse themselves in the rich, lyrical sounds of the Basque language by visiting local festivals, concerts, and cultural events, where the language is embraced and loved.

The Basque Country, with its vivid history, deep-rooted customs, and compelling language, is an amazing location that provides a unique and memorable cultural experience. Biarritz, tucked along the gorgeous Basque coastline, is a good illustration of this diversity, marrying the elegance and refinement of a French resort town with the peculiar Basque tradition that infuses every element of its character.

EXPLORING THE BASQUE ARCHITECTURE AND ART

Biarritz, a picturesque seaside town set along the Basque Country's exquisite coastlines, is a mesmerizing location that not only enchants tourists with its natural beauty but also captivates them with its rich architectural and cultural past.

As a crossroads between French and Basque cultural influences, Biarritz has long been a center of creative expression, where the unique architectural forms and artistic traditions of the Basque people have combined with the beauty and refinement of French architecture. The architectural environment of Biarritz is a patchwork of varied styles, each with its own distinct narrative and cultural importance. One of the most noticeable elements of the town's-built environment is the Basque-influenced architecture, which can be seen in the classic half-timbered homes, the unique red-tiled roofs, and the complex stone masonry that adorns many of the town's old structures.

The Grand Hotel, a grandiose edifice that previously functioned as a refuge for the European aristocracy, is a great example of the Basque-French architectural fusion. Completed in 1893, the hotel's towering front merges Basque and French architectural features, showcasing a massive, symmetrical building with high, pitched roofs and ornate stone carvings that pay respect to the region's rich cultural past.

Another architectural beauty in Biarritz is the Rocher de la Vierge, a spectacular peninsula that juts out into the sea. Atop this distinctive rock formation lies the Église de la Sainte-Vierge, a beautiful Romanesque-style church that dates back to the 19th century. The church's elaborate stone carvings, arched windows, and towering bell tower demonstrate the region's architectural skill and the strong religious and cultural traditions that have defined the Basque identity. Biarritz's artistic past is arguably as rich and varied as its architecture, with a thriving creative community that has always been inspired by the town's natural beauty and Basque cultural traditions. Throughout the town, tourists may find a multitude of art galleries, museums, and public art projects that represent the region's distinct creative heritage.

One of the most known cultural legacies of the Basque Country is the legacy of "Gure Artea," or "Our Art," which spans a broad variety of artistic forms, including painting, sculpture, and textile arts. In Biarritz, this history is honored in several galleries and cultural institutions, where tourists may enjoy the complex, abstract patterns and vivid, earthy color palettes that are characteristics of Basque artistic expression. Another notable component of Biarritz's creative past is the town's long-standing link to the world of fashion. As a trendy resort destination for the European elite, Biarritz has attracted various famous designers and fashion companies, who have taken inspiration from the town's Basque roots and developed iconic items that have become associated with the region's flair and elegance. Biarritz's rich architectural and creative legacy is a monument to the ongoing cultural uniqueness of the Basque people and their ability to smoothly merge their traditions with the influences of the greater French and European artistic landscapes.

GEOGRAPHY AND CLIMATE

Biarritz is located in the Pyrénées-Atlantiques department, inside the Nouvelle-Aquitaine region of France. The town is situated in the Bay of Biscay, a portion of the Atlantic Ocean that runs between the Iberian Peninsula and the west coast of France. This ideal coastal position has played a crucial role in Biarritz's growth since it has given the town access to the sea and a booming marine trade. The town's topography is distinguished by a diversified terrain that smoothly merges cliffs, expansive sandy beaches, and green hinterland regions.

One of the most distinctive topographical features of Biarritz is the Rocher de la Vierge, a dramatic peninsula that juts out into the sea and affords panoramic views of the coastline and the neighboring Basque Country. Another notable physical characteristic of Biarritz is the presence of the Pyrenees Mountains, which constitute the natural boundary between

France and Spain. The town's closeness to these spectacular peaks has not only affected its climate and geography but has also formed the cultural and economic relations between Biarritz and the greater Basque area.

Biarritz features a moderate oceanic environment, with mild temperatures and significant precipitation levels throughout the year. The town's coastline position and closeness to the Pyrenees Mountains contribute to its particular microclimate, which is different from the larger climatic patterns of the Nouvelle-Aquitaine area.

Summers in Biarritz are often warm and sunny, with average temperatures ranging from 20-25°C (68-77°F). The town's coastline location serves to temper the heat, creating a warm and enjoyable summer season that draws people from across the globe. Winters in Biarritz are moderate, with average temperatures often ranging between 10-15°C (50-59°F). While the town does suffer increased quantities of rainfall throughout the winter months, the temperature remains rather mild, with occasional snowfall in the surrounding Pyrenees Mountains. The town's coastline position also adds to its regular exposure to Atlantic weather systems, resulting in a high amount of precipitation throughout the year. This plentiful rainfall helps to support the lush, green landscapes that are distinctive of the Basque Country and also adds to the town's status as a year-round destination for outdoor sports and enjoyment.

Biarritz's unusual geographic position and mild oceanic environment have played a vital part in establishing the town's history, economics, and cultural character. From the dramatic Rocher de la Vierge to the sprawling sandy beaches and the nearby Pyrenees Mountains, Biarritz's diverse and captivating landscape has attracted visitors and residents alike, who have been drawn to the town's natural beauty and the wealth of outdoor activities and recreational opportunities it offers.

As a gateway to the larger Basque Country, Biarritz's strategic location and pleasant climate have also created strong cultural and economic linkages with the surrounding area, adding to the town's rich past and distinctive cultural character. Whether you're attracted to the town's gorgeous landscape, it's warm and temperate weather, or its plethora of outdoor pastimes, Biarritz's distinctive geographic and climatic qualities are guaranteed to make a lasting impact on everyone who visits this amazing coastal resort.

FUN FACTS ABOUT BIARRITZ

Let's look into some of the most intriguing and little-known facts about this unique French town.

1. Royal Retreat: Biarritz's rise to renown as a fashionable vacation location may be primarily traced to the patronage of Napoleon III and his wife, Empress Eugénie. In the 1850s, the imperial couple fell in love with the town's natural beauty and erected a summer palace here, helping to convert Biarritz into a destination for the European elite.

2. Surfing Pioneers: While Biarritz is famed for its magnificent architecture and high-society links, it also has a long history as a pioneering surf destination. In the 1950s, the town became one of the first cities in Europe to embrace the sport of surfing, drawing a growing population of fans from across the globe.

3. Basque Architectural Masterpieces: The town's distinctive architectural style, which blends Basque and

French influences, is showcased in several iconic structures, including the Grand Hotel, a palatial edifice that once hosted royalty and celebrities, and the Rocher de la Vierge, a dramatic promontory crowned by a stunning Romanesque church.

4. Gastronomic Delights: Biarritz's gastronomic scene is a reflection of its Basque history, with local delicacies such as Bayonne ham, Espelette peppers, and Basque cherry cake pleasing the palates of tourists from across the globe. The town is also recognized for its strong seafood sector, with freshly caught fish and shellfish figuring heavily on the menus of its renowned restaurants.

5. Creative Influences: Biarritz has long been a hotspot of creative inspiration, drawing famous painters, sculptors, and fashion designers who have been charmed by the town's natural beauty and rich cultural legacy. The Basque legacy of "Gure Artea," or "Our Art," is honored in several galleries and cultural organizations around the municipality.

6. Pelota Fever: The Basque sport of pelota, a fast-paced handball-like game, is strongly engrained in the local culture, with dedicated courts and eager fans dotting the town's landscape. Visitors may immerse themselves in this centuries-old tradition by witnessing live bouts or even trying their hand at the sport.

7. Oceanographic Museum: Biarritz is home to the Cité de l'Océan et du Surf, a cutting-edge oceanographic museum that gives tourists a fascinating investigation of the aquatic environment and the town's rich nautical heritage. Featuring interactive displays, cutting-edge technology, and spectacular views of the Atlantic Ocean, the museum is a must-visit site for anybody interested in the mysteries of the sea.

From its royal ties and pioneering spirit to its rich cultural legacy and gastronomic pleasures, Biarritz is a town that continuously captivates and surprises.

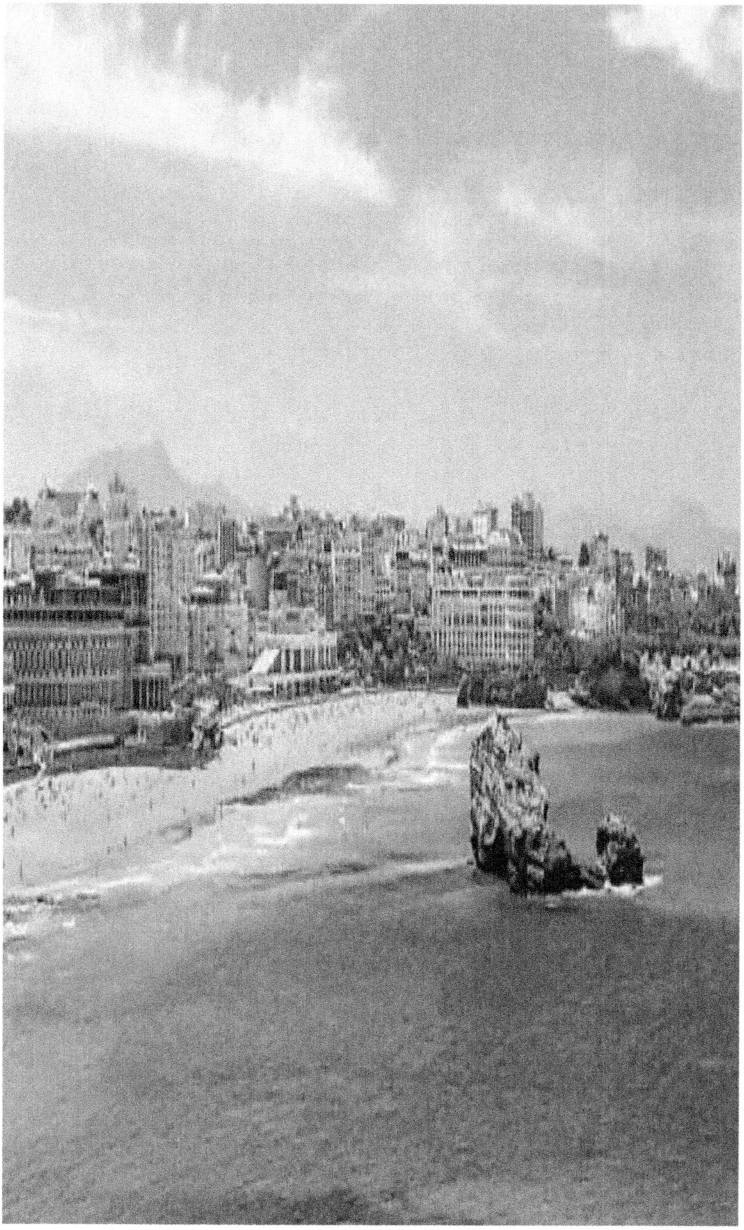

CHAPTER 2

GETTING TO AND NAVIGATING BIARRITZ

AIRPORT INFORMATION

Biarritz Airport, also known as Biarritz-Pays Basque Airport, is an international airport servicing the city of Biarritz and the surrounding Basque area in southern France. The airport is situated roughly 3.5 km (2.2 miles) south of the Biarritz city center, near the village of Anglet. It stands along the Atlantic coast, allowing quick access to the wonderful beaches, coastal villages, and natural landscapes of the Basque Country. There are various transit alternatives available for passengers arriving at or leaving from Biarritz Airport:

I. Taxi: Taxis are widely accessible outside the airport terminal building. Taxi rates to the Biarritz city center normally vary from €15 to €20 for a one-way journey.

II. Shuttle Bus: The Chronoplus shuttle bus line runs a direct service between the airport and Biarritz city center, as well as to other adjacent cities including Bayonne and Anglet. The shuttle operates often and the travel takes roughly 15-20 minutes.

III. Rental Cars: Major car rental firms including Avis, Hertz, and Europcar have offices and pickup locations inside the airport terminal, enabling tourists to simply get a vehicle upon arrival.

IV. Public Transport: For those on a budget, the local bus network run by Chronoplus links the airport to several places in the vicinity. Buses operate often, and a single ticket costs roughly €1.50.

V. Private Transfers: Many hotels and lodging providers in Biarritz and the surrounding region provide private transport services from the airport, which may be requested in advance.

Biarritz Airport has a single terminal building that services both local and international aircraft. The terminal is rather tiny but includes the main facilities and services for travelers:

- **Check-in and Arrivals Halls:** The main check-in desks and baggage claim sections are situated on the ground level of the terminal.

- **Security Screening and Departures Lounge:** Passenger security checkpoints and the departures lounge with boarding gates are placed on the top level.

- **Dining and Shopping:** A range of cafés, restaurants, and duty-free stores can be found inside the departures area, catering to the requirements of travelers.

- **Lounges:** The airport features a VIP lounge accessible for business class passengers and those with airport lounge access.

- **Public Amenities:** Other amenities include free Wi-Fi, ATMs, currency exchange, a tourist information desk, and basic medical care.

Biarritz Airport is equipped with elevators, ramps, and specific parking spots to accommodate guests with decreased mobility or special requirements. The airport mostly handles domestic and regional European destinations. The primary airlines operating at the airport include:

28

- **Air France:** Offering direct flights to Paris-Orly and seasonal links to other French destinations.

- **EasyJet:** Connecting Biarritz to numerous key European cities including London, Amsterdam, and Berlin.

- **Volotea:** Providing seasonal flights to numerous locations in Spain, Italy, and France.

- **Ryanair:** Connecting Biarritz to locations around Europe, including the UK, Ireland, and Italy.

The airport also sees infrequent charter aircraft and private/business aviation activities, notably during the high tourist seasons. Biarritz and the Basque area are popular holiday destinations, especially during the summer months (June to September) when the weather is good, and the beaches are bustling. This is considered the peak season, with greater airline frequency and higher tickets. Other high travel seasons include school vacations (Easter, Christmas) and significant events like the Biarritz Surf Festival and the Fêtes de Bayonne (a famous yearly festival in the adjacent city of Bayonne).

Travelers are urged to book their flights and accommodation well in advance during these busy seasons to ensure the greatest discounts and availability. It is also advisable to arrive at the airport with adequate time to handle the security and boarding procedures, since the terminal may become fairly packed during peak hours.

Biarritz Airport serves as the principal gateway for reaching the attractive Basque area of southern France. With its accessible location, choice of transit options, and basic passenger amenities, the airport delivers a comfortable travel experience for both local and international travelers to this attractive seaside resort.

TRAIN AND BUS SERVICES

Biarritz is well-connected to the French national railway network, providing passengers with easy train connections to explore the area and beyond. SNCF (French National Railway Company) is the major operator of rail services in Biarritz and the neighboring Basque region. The major rail station in Biarritz is the Gare de Biarritz, situated in the city center, only a short walk from the main commercial sector and tourist attractions. Biarritz is serviced by TGV high-speed train services, giving direct links to major French cities including Paris, Bordeaux, and Toulouse. The travel to Paris takes roughly 3.5 hours. In addition to the high-speed TGV, there are frequent intercity and regional train services (TER) that link Biarritz to adjacent towns and cities in the Basque area, such as Bayonne, Hendaye, and San Sebastián in Spain. For longer-distance travel, Biarritz is connected to the Intercités de Nuit (night train) network, providing overnight services to locations including Paris and Marseille.

Tickets for train services in Biarritz may be bought on the SNCF website (www.sncf.com), mobile app, or at the ticket offices situated inside the Gare de Biarritz train station. It is suggested to reserve tickets in advance, particularly for high-speed TGV trains during peak travel seasons, to ensure the best pricing and availability. The train station also includes an information desk where tourists may ask about timetables, routes, and ticket costs. Multilingual personnel are ready to help travelers with their questions. In addition to the substantial rail network, Biarritz and the neighboring Basque area are well-served by a comprehensive bus system, offering a cheap and convenient method of public transit for inhabitants and tourists alike.

Chronoplus is the principal public bus operator in Biarritz and the Basque Country. Chronoplus offers a network of urban and intercity bus lines, linking Biarritz to adjacent towns and cities, including Bayonne, Anglet, and Saint-Jean-de-Luz. Chronoplus provides a comprehensive choice of bus lines that service significant landmarks, retail centers, and transit hubs inside Biarritz, as well as regional routes connecting the city to other Basque locations.

Buses normally operate at regular intervals, with timetables accessible on the Chronoplus website (www.chronoplus.eu). Single-ride tickets for the Chronoplus bus system may be bought directly from the driver or at numerous sales sites, including the Biarritz train station. Discounted multi-ride passes and day tickets are also available for individuals expecting to utilize the buses frequently throughout their stay. In addition to the local Chronoplus buses, Biarritz is serviced by regional and national bus operators, such as Flixbus and Eurolines, which give direct connections to major towns in France, Spain, and beyond.

Long-distance bus services to and from Biarritz normally leave and arrive at the Gare Routière, the city's principal bus terminal, situated near the Gare de Biarritz train station. The bus network in Biarritz and the Basque area is usually accessible, with low-floor buses and allocated places for passengers with restricted mobility or disability. Many buses now provide free Wi-Fi, enabling tourists to remain connected throughout their rides.

The combination of fast rail and bus services in Biarritz and the surrounding region offers tourists a comprehensive and well-integrated public transit system. This enables people to visit the Basque region's gorgeous landscapes, quaint villages, and cultural attractions with ease and cost, making it a very accessible destination for tourists.

CHAPTER 3

ACCOMMODATIONS

HOTELS AND RESORTS OF BIARRITZ

Biarritz has a wide variety of lodging alternatives, ranging from opulent beachfront hotels to quaint boutique establishments, to meet the requirements of every guest. In Biarritz, France, the following are the top ten hotels and resorts in terms of quality:

1. The Hotel du Palais: This property is situated on the famous Grande Plage, which offers a breathtaking view of the Atlantic Ocean. 1 Avenue de l'Impératrice, 64200 Biarritz, France is the address of the establishment. The Hôtel du Palais, which is now considered a historic and landmark hotel, was first constructed as a vacation residence for Napoleon III and Eugénie, who was his wife at the time. The luxury five-star facility in question provides guests with lavish rooms, exquisite dining options, a comprehensive spa, and views of the Biarritz coastline that are unrivaled.

2. Le Regina Biarritz Hotel & Spa: Situated along the Côte des Basques, near to the city center. Address is 52 Avenue de l'Impératrice, 64200 Biarritz, France. A contemporary 5-star hotel that mixes modern luxury with traditional Basque charm. It boasts large accommodations, a

Michelin-starred restaurant, an indoor and outdoor pool, and a state-of-the-art wellness facility.

3. Sofitel Biarritz Le Miramar Thalassa Sea & Spa: Overlooking the Plage du Miramar, within walking distance of the city center. Address is 1 Rue Louison Bobet, 64200 Biarritz, France. This luxurious 5-star resort offers direct access to the beach and features a world-class thalassotherapy spa, an outdoor seawater pool, and a variety of dining options. Guests may enjoy spectacular ocean views from the comfort of their modern rooms and suites.

4. Grand Tonic Hotel Biarritz: Situated in the center of Biarritz, near the Côte des Basques and the city's major attractions. Address is 24 Avenue Edouard VII, 64200 Biarritz, France. A beautiful 4-star boutique hotel that integrates contemporary comforts with traditional Basque architectural aspects. It provides nice apartments, a charming lounge bar, and a rooftop terrace with panoramic views of the city.

5. Radisson Blu Hotel Biarritz: Located on the Côte des Basques, only a short walk from the city center. Address is

1 Rue du Commandant Charcot, 64200 Biarritz, France. A modern 4-star hotel that offers a pleasant and convenient base for visiting Biarritz. It has modern rooms, an outdoor pool, a fitness facility, and an on-site restaurant offering local and foreign cuisine.

6. Hôtel Mercure Biarritz Centre Plaza: Situated in the center of Biarritz, between the Rocher de la Vierge and the Gare de Biarritz train station. Address is 14 Avenue Édouard VII, 64200 Biarritz, France. A contemporary 4-star hotel that provides a pleasant and inexpensive stay in Biarritz. It has well-appointed rooms, a bar, and a breakfast buffet to start the day.

7. Hôtel Beaumanoir: Located in the calm Chiberta sector, a short distance from the city center and the beaches. Address is 2 Rue du Général Foy, 64200 Biarritz, France. A beautiful 4-star boutique hotel that mixes traditional Basque architecture with modern decor. It offers a heated outdoor pool, a spa center, and a restaurant highlighting local Basque cuisine.

8. Hôtel La Marisa: Situated along the Côte des Basques, with direct access to the beac. Address: 12 Avenue de la Marna, 64200 Biarritz, France. A family-run 3-star hotel that provides a pleasant and inviting environment. Guests may enjoy spectacular ocean views, a sun deck, and easy access to the beach and adjacent attractions.

9. Hôtel Edouard VII: Located in the center of Biarritz, only a short walk from the Rocher de la Vierge and the Biarritz Casino. Address is 8 Avenue Edouard VII, 64200 Biarritz, France. A beautiful 3-star hotel that mixes Basque culture with contemporary amenities. It has pleasant accommodations, a nice lounge bar, and a handy location for experiencing Biarritz's attractions.

10. Résidence Hôtelière Arcé: Situated in the Chiberta neighborhood, a short distance from the beach and the city center. Address is 47 Rue de la Concorde, 64200 Biarritz, France. A 3-star aparthotel that offers self-catering rooms, excellent for families or prolonged visits. It provides a choice of studio and apartment-style apartments, as well as on-site facilities including a swimming pool and a fitness center.

These hotels and resorts in Biarritz provide a broad choice of accommodations to meet the interests and budgets of various guests.

UNIQUE BOUTIQUE STAYS AND VACATION RENTALS

1. Villa Eugénie: Situated in the center of Biarritz, only a short walk from the Rocher de la Vierge and the Grand Plage. Address is 8 Rue Eugénie, 64200 Biarritz, France. Villa Eugénie is a gorgeous 19th-century estate that has been meticulously repaired and turned into a luxury 5-room boutique hotel. Exuding Basque charm and stylish refinement, the villa gives visitors a genuinely immersive and customized experience, with tastefully fitted rooms, a tranquil garden, and outstanding service.

2. Maison Estella: Located in the lovely Chiberta quarter, a short distance from the ocean and the city center. Address is 11 Rue Edmond Rostand, 64200 Biarritz, France. Maison Estella is a sleek and contemporary boutique guesthouse that mixes Basque tradition with modern design. Featuring only 6 guest rooms, this compact facility provides a tranquil and customized refuge, replete with a stunning garden, a warm lounge, and a delicious breakfast patio.

3. La Maison Biarritz: Situated in the heart of the Biarritz city center, within walking distance of the Plage du Miramar and the Côte des Basques. Address is 5 Rue Gambetta, 64200 Biarritz, France. La Maison Biarritz is a modern and refined boutique hotel that pays respect to the city's rich heritage and Basque character. With only 8 guest rooms, this facility provides a unique and personal experience, replete with attentive facilities, a delightful courtyard, and a wonderfully chosen design sense.

4. Apartment Rental: Villa Chiberta: Situated in the Chiberta sector, a tranquil and exclusive residential area near the beach. Address is 1 Impasse Edmond Rostand, 64200 Biarritz, France. For guests wanting more autonomous and spacious lodging, Villa Chiberta provides a selection of nicely decorated vacation rental apartments. These self-catering flats, ranging from studios to multi-bedroom apartments, give visitors with the comforts of home, contemporary conveniences, and easy access to the neighboring beaches and activities.

5. Apartment Rental: Biarritz Côte des Basques: Located along the famed Côte des Basques, with direct access to the beach and spectacular ocean views. Address is 12 Avenue de la Marna, 64200 Biarritz, France. Biarritz Côte des Basques is a collection of premium vacation rental apartments that provide a unique seaside experience. Ranging from studio units to spacious multi-bedroom apartments, these elegantly designed accommodations provide guests with the perfect base to immerse themselves in the Basque coastal lifestyle, with private terraces, modern amenities, and easy access to renowned surf spots and beach promenades.

These distinctive boutique stays and vacation homes in Biarritz provide tourists with a more intimate and customized experience compared to regular hotels. From ancient palaces and quaint guesthouses to luxurious seaside apartments, these properties give visitors a closer connection to the Basque culture, spectacular natural surroundings, and the overall spirit of Biarritz.

AIRBNB AND VACATION RENTALS

For guests seeking more customized and unique lodgings during their time in Biarritz, the city offers a large range of Airbnb and vacation rental choices. From comfortable flats to gorgeous villas, these alternative lodgings give a home-away-from-home feel and typically come with unique facilities and personal touches.

1. Luxury Beachfront Villa with Panoramic Views: Situated right on the Côte des Basques, with unimpeded views of the Atlantic Ocean. Address is 1 Rue de la Côte des Basques, 64200 Biarritz, France. This beautiful 4-bedroom home provides the best in luxury and seclusion. Featuring a private pool, a big patio, and contemporary, open-concept decor, the villa can easily accommodate up to 8 people. Guests may enjoy direct access to the beach and spectacular sunsets over the ocean.

2. Charming Basque-Style Apartment in the City Center: Located in the center of Biarritz, only a short walk from the Rocher de la Vierge and the major retail district. Address is 14 Rue Gambetta, 64200 Biarritz, France. This tiny 2-bedroom apartment reflects the spirit of Basque architecture and decor. With its classic wooden beams, colorful accents, and well-appointed conveniences, the apartment can house up to 4 people and offers a comfortable base for exploring Biarritz on foot.

3. Hillside Villa with Panoramic Views: Perched on a hilltop in the Chiberta neighborhood, affording breathtaking panoramas of the Basque coastline. Address is 25 Rue des Bruyères, 64200 Biarritz, France. This 3-bedroom home is a sanctuary of solitude, with a verdant garden, a private pool, and stunning views of the Atlantic Ocean. The villa can sleep up to 6 people and offers a private getaway, while being within a short distance of Biarritz's major attractions.

4. Chic Loft-Style Apartment near the Beach: Located in the Côte des Basques district, only a 5-minute walk from the beach. Address is 8 Rue du Commandant Charcot, 64200 Biarritz, France. This sleek and spacious 1-bedroom loft apartment is excellent for couples or lone travelers. With its open-plan layout, elegant decor, and private balcony, the apartment provides a fashionable and pleasant stay, only a stone's throw away from the Biarritz beach.

5. Cozy Seaside Cottage: Set in the quiet Chiberta neighborhood, a short drive from the city center and the beaches. Address is 17 Rue des Bruyères, 64200 Biarritz, France. This beautiful 2-bedroom home gives a tranquil and traditional Basque experience for up to 4 people. The cottage offers a well-equipped kitchen, a pleasant living room, and a private garden, giving an ideal getaway for those seeking a more local and immersive stay in Biarritz.

These Airbnb and vacation rental choices in Biarritz give guests a broad selection of lodgings, from magnificent beachfront villas to modest Basque-style flats. It's crucial to note that, as with any vacation rental, it's suggested to carefully study the property's listing, facilities, and ratings before booking to verify it matches your expectations and needs. Additionally, be sure to acquaint yourself with the check-in/check-out processes, any unique house regulations, and the surrounding neighborhood to make the most of your time in Biarritz.

CAMPING OPTIONS

For those wanting a more adventurous and nature-oriented experience in the Basque region of France, Biarritz offers an assortment of fantastic camping possibilities. From beachside campgrounds to stunning rural getaways, the region around Biarritz gives numerous alternatives for those who want to immerse themselves in the great outdoors. Here are the best 5 camping choices in Biarritz, France:

1. Camping Atalaye: Situated right on the Côte des Basques, with breathtaking views of the Atlantic Ocean. Address is 180 Avenue de la Plage, 64200 Biarritz, France. Camping Atalaye is a 4-star campground that gives direct access to the gorgeous Côte des Basques beach. It provides fully-equipped campsites with electricity connections, as well as mobile home rentals for those who want a more pleasant camping experience. Facilities include a swimming pool, a snack bar, and a range of recreational activities, making it a perfect option for families and outdoor lovers.

2. Camping Txiki-Camping: Set in the quiet countryside, only a 10-minute drive from the Biarritz city center. Address is 9 Chemin de Langardia, 64200 Biarritz, France.

Camping Txiki-Camping is a delightful 4-star campground that provides a tranquil and natural environment, surrounded by rolling hills and rich greenery. The park has wide spaces for tents, caravans, and motorhomes, as well as mobile home rentals. Amenities include a swimming pool, a bar, a restaurant, and a playground, providing the requirements of both families and couples.

3. Camping Ilbarritz: Situated along the Côte des Basques, only a short walk from the Plage de la Milady beach. Address is 1 Chemin de Sainte Barbe, 64200 Biarritz, France. Camping Ilbarritz is a 4-star campground that combines a fantastic beachside setting with a broad selection of services and activities. Campers may select from well-equipped plots or choose for mobile home rentals. The campground has an outdoor swimming pool, a wellness area, a sports field, and a range of food and entertainment choices, making it an excellent spot for an active and pleasurable camping holiday.

4. Camping Erretegia: Set in a calm natural environment, about 15 minutes from the Biarritz city center. Address is 15 Chemin de Lascoumettes, 64200 Biarritz, France.

Camping Erretegia is a 3-star campground that provides a calm and attractive atmosphere, surrounded by thick pine trees and undulating hills. The park has wide spaces for tents, caravans, and motorhomes, as well as mobile home rentals. Facilities include an outdoor swimming pool, a children's play area, a bar, and a small grocery shop, catering to the requirements of families and nature lovers.

5. Camping Chiberta: Located in the Chiberta neighborhood, only a short distance from the Plage de la Milady and the Biarritz city center. Address is 42 Chemin de Chiberta, 64200 Biarritz, France. Camping Chiberta is a 3-star campground that provides a more urban camping experience, with easy access to the services and attractions of Biarritz. The park includes spaces for tents, caravans, and motorhomes, as well as mobile home rentals. Facilities include an outdoor swimming pool, a snack bar, and a sports field, making it a handy alternative for people who want to be near the city while still enjoying the great outdoors.

These camping alternatives in Biarritz provide a broad variety of experiences, from beachside campgrounds to tranquil rural getaways.

CHAPTER 4

CULINARY DELIGHTS

BASQUE CUISINE

Basque cuisine is a unique combination of French and Spanish culinary influences, reflecting the region's location straddling the border between the two nations. The Basque people, known as the Euskaldunak, have a strong cultural identity that is strongly connected with their traditional culinary techniques and ingredients.

The region's closeness to the sea is a defining aspect of Basque cuisine, with an abundance of fresh seafood, such as cod, tuna, anchovies, and the famous Bayonne ham, playing a prominent role. Additionally, the lush Basque Country is recognized for its high-quality agricultural output, including peppers, tomatoes, beans, and numerous vegetables. When visiting Biarritz, guests may immerse themselves in the unique tastes of Basque cuisine by indulging in the following characteristic dishes and specialties:

1. Pintxos: The Basque equivalent of Spanish tapas, pintxos are little, bite-sized nibbles that are often served on a piece of bread or skewered. These savory concoctions generally use local items like shellfish, aged meats, and cheeses.

2. Gâteau Basque: A famous Basque delicacy, the Gâteau Basque is a rich, buttery cake filled with either a creamy custard or black cherry compote. It's a renowned local dish that can be found at bakeries and cafés around Biarritz.

3. Axoa: A classic Basque stew cooked with finely diced veal or beef, onions, and peppers, sometimes seasoned with paprika and other fragrant spices. Axoa is often eaten with rice or crusty bread.

4. Lamb meals: The Basque area is recognized for its outstanding quality lamb, and Biarritz provides a range of lamb-based meals, such as grilled lamb chops, lamb stew, and the distinctive Basque-style lamb chops known as Kotonak.

5. Seafood Specialties: Biarritz's seaside location gives an abundance of fresh seafood, which is presented in local dishes including grilled or sautéed fish, fish stews, and the traditional Basque fish soup called Marmitako.

Beyond the characteristic dishes, Biarritz's culinary sector provides a varied choice of eating experiences that enable tourists to immerse themselves in the Basque culture and customs.

Pintxo Hopping: Exploring the city's colorful pintxo bars and enjoying a range of these little meals is a characteristic Basque experience. Visitors may go on self-guided pintxo excursions or join organized culinary walks to explore the greatest local places.

Cider Houses (Sidrerias): The Basque area is famed for its superb cider, and visiting a traditional cider house is a must-do experience. These convivial venues provide locally made cider, frequently combined with robust Basque meals and a boisterous environment.

Gastronomic Experiences: Biarritz is home to many Michelin-starred restaurants and recognized chefs who exhibit the region's best ingredients and culinary methods. Visitors may indulge in tasting meals, culinary lessons, and other immersive gourmet experiences.

Artisanal Food Products: The Basque Country is recognized for its high-quality artisanal food products, such as Espelette peppers, Ossau-Iraty cheese, and the famed

Bayonne ham. Travelers may visit local markets, food stores, and producers to explore and acquire these delights.

Embracing the Basque culinary culture is a vital element of any visit to Biarritz, allowing guests a genuine experience of the region's rich cultural past and the remarkable quality of its native products and cuisine.

MUST-TRY DISHES AND LOCAL SPECIALTIES

1. Pintxos (Basque-style Tapas): Pintxos are the Basque Country's equivalent of Spanish tapas, little bite-sized appetizers often served on a slice of bread or impaled with a toothpick. These tasty and artistically stunning appetizers are a crucial component of the local culinary culture. In Biarritz, travelers may explore the city's numerous pintxos bars, experiencing a range of unique cocktails utilizing ingredients like anchovies, Idiazábal cheese, roasted peppers, and cured meats.

2. Axoa d'Espelette: Axoa is a classic Basque stew cooked with finely chopped or minced beef, bell peppers, and the famed Espelette pepper, a favorite local item recognized for its mild, slightly smokey taste. This substantial and cozy meal is a staple in Biarritz and is commonly served with crusty bread or Basque-style rice.

3. Gâteau Basque: The Gâteau Basque is a famous regional delicacy that has become a symbol of Basque culinary pride. This delightful dessert has a buttery, shortbread-like crust filled with either a creamy vanilla custard or a luscious black cherry jam. It's the ideal complement to a cup of strong Basque coffee or a glass of Basque cider.

4. Morue à la Biscayenne (Biscayan-style Cod): As a seaside town, Biarritz is famed for its superb seafood, and one of the most recognizable local specialties is Morue à la Biscayenne. This meal comprises fresh cod made in the Biscayan way, which often entails boiling the fish in a tasty tomato-based sauce with peppers, onions, and garlic.

5. Ttoro (Basque Fish Stew): Ttoro is a classic Basque fisherman's stew prepared with a variety of fresh local seafood, such as hake, cod, and anchovies, cooked in a thick, tomato-based broth. This rich and comforting meal is a reflection of the region's close relationship to the sea and its bountiful marine resources.

6. Foie Gras: While not entirely a Basque delicacy, the cultivation of high-quality foie gras is a source of pride in the Biarritz area, which is noted for its beautiful farmlands and diversified agricultural offers. Visitors may enjoy wonderful foie gras dishes, either as a single delicacy or blended with other local delicacies.

7. Marmitako (Tuna and Potato Stew): Marmitako is a classic Basque tuna and potato stew that is especially popular in Biarritz and the neighboring coastal districts. This tasty and comforting meal mixes fresh tuna, potatoes, onions, and peppers in a rich broth, frequently seasoned with paprika and other Basque spices.

8. Seafood Platters: Biarritz's great position on the Atlantic coast offers it access to an abundance of fresh fish, and the city's restaurants regularly exhibit this wealth with outstanding seafood platters. These platters may feature a variety of oysters, shrimp, crab, lobster, and other seasonal products, enabling visitors to enjoy the region's unique and high-quality marine delicacies. These are just a handful of the must-try meals and local delicacies that exemplify the rich culinary traditions of Biarritz and the Basque Country. By experiencing the city's lively culinary scene, guests can immerse themselves in the distinct tastes and cultural traditions that make this seaside destination a genuine gourmet joy.

RENOWNED RESTAURANTS AND CAFÉS

Biarritz is famed not just for its magnificent coastline and exquisite architecture but also for its great food scene. From Michelin-starred fine dining restaurants to quaint neighborhood cafés, Biarritz provides a vast selection of eating alternatives that appeal to a wide range of tastes and interests. Here are some of the most known restaurants and cafés in Biarritz that tourists can explore:

1. Le Café de l'Océan:
- o   Type: Fine Dining Restaurant.
- o   Location: 1 Quai de la Négresse, 64200 Biarritz, France.

Situated right on the oceanfront, this 2-Michelin-starred restaurant provides stunning views of the Atlantic Ocean and a menu that displays the finest of Basque and French cuisine. Under the guidance of famed chef Arnaud Lallement, the restaurant delivers a sophisticated and unique dining experience.

2. La Marée:
- Type: Seafood Restaurant.
- Location: 22 Avenue de la Marne, 64200 Biarritz, France.

As the name implies, La Marée focuses on fresh, locally sourced seafood. This family-run restaurant is famous for its superb service, informal but sophisticated decor, and cuisine that embraces the wealth of the Basque coast, from grilled oysters to bouillabaisse.

3. Le Café des Arts:
- Type: Brasserie.
- Location: 2 Place Clemenceau, 64200 Biarritz, France.

A lovely brasserie located in the center of Biarritz; Le Café des Arts provides a typical French dining experience.

From substantial plats du jour to handmade drinks, this boisterous business is a favorite with residents and travelers alike, recognized for its friendly welcome and dynamic environment.

4. Le Clos Basque:
- Type: Traditional Basque Cuisine.
- Location: 8 Rue Mazagran, 64200 Biarritz, France.

For a real flavor of Basque culture, Le Clos Basque is the place to go. This quaint restaurant specializes in traditional Basque foods, from pintxos (Basque tapas) to substantial stews and grilled meats, all cooked using locally sourced ingredients and time-honored methods.

5. Le Café de la Paix:
- Type: Café and Pastry Shop.
- Location: 20 Avenue de la Marne, 64200 Biarritz, France.

A typical French café with a gorgeous Belle Époque-style décor, Le Café de la Paix is a favorite location for visitors and residents alike. Known for its scrumptious pastries, handmade bread, and rich, fragrant coffee, it's the ideal location to indulge in a moment of Parisian-style calm.

6. Le Café des Corsaires:
- o   Type: Casual Bistro.
- o   Location: 9 Rue du Port Vieux, 64200 Biarritz, France.

Overlooking the scenic Port Vieux in Biarritz, this informal cafe provides a mellow and sociable ambiance. The menu comprises substantial Basque-influenced meals, from grilled meat and seafood to regional favorites like piperade and axoa, all accompanied by a well-chosen selection of local wines.

7. La Grange:
- o   Type: Farm-to-Table Restaurant.
- o   Location: Chemin de Latapy, 64200 Biarritz, France.

Situated just outside the city center, La Grange is a farm-to-table restaurant that highlights the finest of the Basque region's seasonal and organic products. With an emphasis on sustainable and locally sourced products, the cuisine delivers a sophisticated and flavor-driven dining experience in a lovely, rustic environment.

8. Le Café de Miremont:
- Type: Café and Patisserie.
- Location: 11 Rue Gambetta, 64200 Biarritz, France.

A Biarritz tradition going back to 1872, Le Café de Miremont is a typical French café noted for its beautiful pastries, delightful hot chocolates, and gorgeous Belle Époque-style décor. It's a renowned destination for indulging in a sweet treat and taking up the historic aura of the city.

These are just a handful of the numerous famous restaurants and cafés that make Biarritz a gastronomic destination in its own right.

PINTXOS CRAWL

Pintxos (pronounced "peen-chos") are the Basque variant of tapas, little delicious pieces that are often served on a slice of bread or impaled with a toothpick. These bite-sized delights are a mainstay of Basque cuisine and have become a vital component of the social and gastronomic experience in Biarritz and the surrounding area. Embarking on a Pintxos Crawl in Biarritz is comparable to a gastronomic expedition, where guests may jump from one typical Basque bar or "Pintxos bar" to the next, savoring a broad assortment of these exquisite morsels. The experience is as much about the cuisine as it is about the vibrant environment and the opportunity to mix with the people. The selection of Pintxos offered in Biarritz is astounding, reflecting the ingenuity and culinary competence of the local chefs and bartenders. Some of the most frequent and appreciated Pintxos include:

- **Gilda:** A typical Pintxos prepared of a green olive, a pickled guindilla pepper, and a salty anchovy, all impaled on a toothpick.

- **Txistorra:** A sort of spicy Basque sausage, generally eaten grilled and coupled with a piece of bread.

- **Tortilla Española:** The quintessential Spanish omelet, generally served in bite-sized pieces.

- **Bacalao:** Salted and dried fish, served in different ways, such as in a creamy sauce or fried.

- **Pimientos de Padrón:** Small green peppers, gently cooked and dusted with coarse sea salt.

- **Idiazabal Cheese:** A typical Basque sheep's milk cheese, frequently eaten with membrillo (quince paste).

When beginning on a Pintxos Crawl in Biarritz, the experience normally proceeds as follows:

- Start your adventure on the vibrant Rue Gambetta, the hub of the city's Pintxos bar scene, where you'll discover a high concentration of these places.

- Hop from one pub to the next, enjoying a Pintxos or two at each stop, accompanied by a drink of local wine, cider, or a crisp Basque beer.

- Engage with the bartenders and locals, who are typically happy to give their advice and insights into the Basque culinary traditions.

- Pace yourself, since the Pintxos Crawl is supposed to be a leisurely and convivial event, letting you taste the flavors and absorb the colorful environment. Explore the neighboring neighborhoods and side streets, as you may stumble into hidden gem Pintxos bars that provide distinct regional delicacies.

LOCAL MARKETS AND FOOD FESTIVALS

1. **Biarritz Farmer's Market (Marché des Halles de Biarritz):**
   - **Address:** Place Sainte-Eugénie, 64200 Biarritz, France.
   - **Operating Hours:** Tuesdays, Thursdays, and Saturdays from 7:00 AM to 1:00 PM.

Located in the center of Biarritz, near the Gare de Biarritz rail station, this classic indoor and outdoor farmer's market is a nexus for local growers, craftsmen, and food aficionados. Visitors may discover a great assortment of fresh fruit, meats, cheeses, seafood, baked products, and regional delicacies from the Basque Country. It's the ideal spot to immerse yourself in the local culinary culture and stock up on high-quality ingredients.

2. **Biarritz Covered Market (Halles de Biarritz):**
   - **Address:** Place Sainte-Eugénie, 64200 Biarritz, France.

- **Operating Hours:** Monday to Saturday, 7:00 AM to 1:00 PM.

Adjacent to the Biarritz Farmer's Market, in the city center, the Biarritz Covered Market is a historic indoor marketplace that has been running since the late 19th century. It features a diversified variety of booths selling a wide range of local and regional goods, including fresh vegetables, meat, seafood, cheese, delicatessen items, and artisanal crafts. The market's bustling atmosphere and vivid exhibits create a stimulating shopping experience for tourists.

3. **Biarritz Flea Market (Marché aux Puces de Biarritz):**
    - **Address:** Rue de la Concorde, 64200 Biarritz, France.
    - **Operating Hours:** Sundays from 8:00 AM to 1:00 PM (seasonal, normally from March to October).

Held in the Chiberta neighborhood, on the outskirts of Biarritz, the Biarritz Flea Market is a famous weekly event that draws residents and visitors alike in quest of unusual antiques, vintage things, collectibles, and second-hand treasures. Browsing the booths and bargaining with the friendly merchants may be a fascinating experience for those seeking one-of-a-kind items.

4. Biarritz Surf Festival: Held annually in July, highlighting the town's strong surfing legacy, this colorful festival promotes the finest of Basque cuisine, with an emphasis on local seafood and grilled delicacies. Visitors may enjoy live music, cooking demos, and a vibrant environment while they partake in the region's wonderful gastronomic delights.

5. Fêtes de Bayonne: Held yearly in late July to early August, in the adjacent city of Bayonne, the Fêtes de Bayonne is one of the biggest and most renowned events in the Basque Country, drawing millions of tourists each year. While the festival's major focus is on cultural traditions, music, and entertainment, it also contains a heavy emphasis on local food. Visitors may browse a variety of food booths, try regional cuisines, and immerse themselves in the lively Basque gastronomic culture.

6. Basque Country Gastronomic Festival (Euskal Jaiak): Held annually in September, honoring the gastronomic traditions of the Basque area, this festival promotes a great variety of Basque cuisine, with a special emphasis on traditional recipes, artisanal goods, and local producers. Visitors may attend cooking demos, partake in tastings, and connect with the enthusiastic local chefs and food artisans who maintain the region's culinary heritage.

These local markets and food festivals in Biarritz and the surrounding Basque region provide guests with a unique chance to experience the famous culinary skill and artisanal spirit of the area. By immersing themselves in these dynamic events, visitors may explore the tastes, ingredients, and traditions that make the Basque Country a recognized gastronomy destination.

CHAPTER 5

TOP ATTRACTIONS AND SIGHTS

THE ICONIC BIARRITZ BEACH AND PROMENADE

The Biarritz Beach, also known as the Grande Plage, is the city's major beach, situated in the center of Biarritz, immediately in front of the historic Hôtel du Palais. Stretching along the Côte des Basques, the Grande Plage is bordered by the vibrant Promenade des Anglais, a busy coastal promenade that serves as the social and economic core of Biarritz. The beach and promenade are located in the city's center region, within easy walking distance of the major retail districts, restaurants, and other popular attractions including the Rocher de la Vierge and the Biarritz Casino. The Biarritz Beach and Promenade provide an assortment of facilities and services to cater to the demands of visitors:

Beach Access and Facilities: The Grande Plage gives direct access to the Atlantic Ocean, with lifeguards on duty throughout the peak summer season to protect the safety of swimmers and beachgoers. Various beach amenities, including showers, changing rooms, and rental equipment (umbrellas, sunbeds, etc.), are provided.

Promenade stores and Restaurants: The Promenade des Anglais is lined with a broad assortment of stores, boutiques, cafés, and restaurants, providing everything from native Basque cuisine to international delicacies. Visitors may enjoy a leisurely walk while perusing the unique items.

In addition to swimming and sunbathing, Biarritz Beach and Promenade give chances for numerous sports, such as surfing, stand-up paddle boarding, and beach volleyball, appealing to the energetic and adventurous tourist. While the beach and promenade are very walkable, there are various public parking choices nearby for those coming by vehicle. The region is also well-connected to the city's public transit network, with the Biarritz train station and bus terminal situated close.

Throughout the year, the Biarritz Beach and Promenade hosts a variety of events, festivals, and cultural festivities, including the famed Biarritz Surf Festival, which attracts surfers and spectators from across the globe. The Biarritz Beach and Promenade suffer considerable swings in visitor numbers and activity levels throughout the year:

- **Summer (June to September):** This is the peak season when the beach and promenade come alive with sunbathers, swimmers, and a dynamic atmosphere. Water sports, beach bars, and numerous events and festivals take place throughout this season.

- **Shoulder Seasons (Spring and Fall):** The beach and promenade remain open and accessible, however with fewer people and a more relaxed attitude. Water temperatures may be colder, but the landscape and beach excursions are still delightful.

- **Winter (November to February):** While the beach is normally less popular during the winter months, the promenade and neighboring attractions, such as the Biarritz Casino, remain open, giving a more serene experience for tourists.

Visitors to the Biarritz Beach and Promenade should be careful of the following regulations and etiquette:

- Respect the specified swimming and bathing areas, as indicated by the lifeguards.

- Dispose of garbage and waste appropriately in the supplied containers to keep the area clean.
- Refrain from noisy or disruptive conduct, especially in the calmer portions of the promenade.
- Be attentive to others and keep the paths clean for pedestrian traffic.
- Obey any signs or instructions supplied by the local authorities.

The Biarritz Beach and Promenade are the heart and soul of this historic French Basque resort town, providing tourists with a unique combination of natural beauty, dynamic atmosphere, and limitless chances for leisure, recreation, and cultural participation.

THE ROCHER DE LA VIERGE

The Rocher de la Vierge is situated on the southern end of Biarritz's shoreline, only a short walk from the city center. The simplest approach to visit the property is by following the magnificent seaside promenade that runs along the Plage de la Côte des Basques. Alternatively, you may climb the steps or the old footbridge that goes straight to the rock formation. The Rocher de la Vierge has been an intrinsic part of Biarritz's history and character for generations. In the 19th century, a statue of the Virgin Mary was constructed atop the rock, which was subsequently linked to the mainland by a wooden footbridge. This footbridge, known as the Passerelle de la Vierge, allows people to easily ascend the cliff and observe the beautiful views of the Atlantic Ocean. Over time, the wooden footbridge was rebuilt with a more robust iron structure, which still exists today, giving a distinctive and dramatic access point to the Rocher de la Vierge. Visiting the Rocher de la Vierge is a wonderfully engaging experience. As you cross the footbridge and reach the summit of the rock, you'll be met with spectacular panoramic views of the Biarritz coastline, the pounding waves, and the immense expanse of the Atlantic Ocean. Here are some of the important features and activities you may enjoy at the Rocher de la Vierge:

I. Admire the Stunning Coastal Scenery: Take in the sweeping panoramas of the Biarritz coastline, the renowned Villa Belza, and the beautiful waves pouring in from the open sea. It's a genuinely stunning sight that will leave a lasting impact.

II. Explore the Statue of the Virgin Mary: At the highest point of the Rocher de la Vierge, you'll discover the statue of the Virgin Mary, a symbol of the site's religious and cultural importance.

III. Visit the Lighthouse: Adjacent to the Rocher de la Vierge, you'll discover a historic lighthouse that gives extra panoramic views of the coastline. Visitors may examine the lighthouse's exterior and learn about its function in directing ships and seafarers.

IV. Enjoy the Promenade and Beach: The Rocher de la Vierge is bordered by the gorgeous coastal promenade, which is great for strolls and taking in the views. You may also reach the neighboring Plage de la Côte des Basques, one of Biarritz's famed surfing beaches.

To guarantee the safety and preservation of the Rocher de la Vierge, there are a few restrictions and regulations that visitors should be aware of:

- Access to the Rocher de la Vierge is free, however the footbridge and adjacent areas may be restricted during severe weather or for repair.

- Visitors are encouraged to use care while crossing the footbridge and to avoid wandering too near to the edge of the rock structure.

- Swimming, climbing, or indulging in any harmful activity on the Rocher de la Vierge is completely banned.

- Pets are permitted on the property; however, they must be kept on a leash at all times. Respectful conduct and compliance with any on-site directives from personnel or signage is expected.

The Rocher de la Vierge is available to the public year-round, with the following working hours: Summer (May to September): 7:00 AM to 8:00 PM, and Winter (October to April): 8:00 AM to 6:00 PM. It's essential to remember that the facility may be closed or have limited hours during severe weather or for special events, so it's always a good idea to check the latest information before your visit. This renowned monument provides a unique combination of natural beauty, historical importance, and spectacular coastline views that will certainly have a lasting effect on your journey to this lovely French Basque resort.

THE BIARRITZ LIGHTHOUSE

As a prime tourism destination in southern France, Biarritz is recognized for its gorgeous Atlantic coastline, rich Basque history, and iconic monuments. Prominently standing atop the dramatic cliffs overlooking the crashing waves, the Biarritz Lighthouse (Phare de Biarritz) is one of the city's most renowned and visited attractions, offering travelers a unique opportunity to experience panoramic views, explore the region's maritime history, and immerse themselves in the captivating natural beauty of the Basque Country.

The Biarritz Lighthouse is situated at the northern extremity of the Côte des Basques, only a short walk from the city center. The lighthouse rests atop the Pointe Saint-Martin, a rocky peninsula that juts out into the Atlantic Ocean, giving it a commanding presence over the surrounding shoreline. Visitors may approach the lighthouse by following the well-marked pedestrian pathways and walkways from the neighboring beach areas and promenade. The trip to the summit entails mounting a flight of steps, therefore the site may not be accessible for persons with mobility issues. The Biarritz Lighthouse has a long history stretching back to the

19th century. The present building was erected in 1834, replacing a previous lighthouse that had fallen into ruin. Designed in the classical style, the lighthouse tower rises at a height of 73 meters (240 feet), making it one of the highest on the French Atlantic coast.

Over the years, the lighthouse has acted as a crucial navigational aid for sailors traveling the dangerous seas of the Basque area. It was completely automated in 1991, reducing the need for a permanent team of lighthouse keepers. Today, the lighthouse continues to direct mariners along the coastline, while simultaneously acting as a treasured icon and tourism attraction for tourists to Biarritz. Visiting the Biarritz Lighthouse provides guests with a unique and rewarding experience. Upon arrival, guests are met with the majestic sight of the lighthouse rising above the rocky cliffs, with amazing views of the Atlantic Ocean and the surrounding Basque region.

Guided tours of the lighthouse's interior are provided, enabling visitors to ascend the spiral staircase to the top of the tower, where they may enjoy panoramic sights of the Biarritz coastline and the distant Pyrenees mountains.

During the tour, guests may learn about the lighthouse's history, its function in marine navigation, and the technology that powers its beacons. The area around the lighthouse is covered by a network of picturesque coastal paths and pathways, providing tourists the chance to explore the magnificent Basque cliffs, watch the crashing waves, and take in the stunning natural beauty of the region.

The Biarritz Lighthouse and its surrounding cliffs are a popular site for birdwatchers, who come to observe a variety of seabirds, including gulls, cormorants, and the odd peregrine falcon. One of the most popular times to visit the Biarritz Lighthouse is during the golden hour, when the setting sun spreads a warm light over the shoreline, producing a spectacular visual spectacle. To protect the safety and maintenance of the Biarritz Lighthouse, visitors are required to comply with the following laws and regulations:

o **Guided Tours:** Access to the inside of the lighthouse is only authorized via a guided tour, which may be scheduled in advance or upon arrival.

- **Accessibility:** The lighthouse's spiral stairway may provide obstacles for visitors with mobility impairments or those who are uncomfortable with heights.

- **Photography:** Visitors are allowed to take photos, but the use of tripods and other equipment that might impede paths is banned.

- **Pets:** Pets are normally not permitted inside the lighthouse premises, except for service animals.

The lighthouse and its surrounding grounds are available to the public during daylight hours, normally from 10:00 AM to 6:00 PM, with final admission permitted around one hour before closure. To get the most out of your visit to the Biarritz Lighthouse, it's advisable to organize your trip in advance. Check the lighthouse's official website or ask local tourist offices for the latest information on tour schedules, entrance prices, and any seasonal or weather-related closures. Don't forget to wear comfortable walking shoes, pack sun protection, and dress properly for the seaside weather, which may be extremely unpredictable. Combine your lighthouse visit with a walk down the surrounding promenade, a stop at one of the delightful Basque cafés, or a day spent exploring the other natural and cultural treasures that make Biarritz such a wonderful location.

THE BIARRITZ CASINO

The Biarritz Casino stands as a real symbol, captivating people from across the globe with its unrivaled beauty, rich history, and exhilarating adventures. As a major attraction in the picturesque coastal town of Biarritz, this spectacular business guarantees to be the highlight of any visit to the area.

The Biarritz Casino, initially completed in 1901, is a real architectural gem, integrating aspects of Baroque, Belle Époque, and Basque-inspired architecture. Designed by the famous architect Édouard-Jean Niermans, the building's magnificent façade, embellished with elaborate carvings and sculptures, quickly grabs the attention of anyone who sets eyes upon it. Step inside the magnificent entryway, and you'll be taken back in time, marveling at the rich interiors, boasting extravagant chandeliers, beautiful moldings, and gorgeous stained-glass windows.

At the heart of the Biarritz Casino lies its world-famous gaming tables, offering guests a chance to enjoy a thrilling choice of traditional casino games. From the thrill of roulette and blackjack to the fascinating attraction of slot machines, the casino caters to every sort of gaming fan.

But the Biarritz Casino is much more than simply a gambling attraction. It also features a bustling entertainment program, offering live music, cabaret performances, and other cultural events that exhibit the rich legacy of the Basque area. From the luxury of the Grand Salon to the stylish atmosphere of the Café des Sports, the casino provides a broad selection of eating and socializing alternatives, appealing to every taste and desire.

As with any famous casino, the Biarritz Casino maintains a set of regulations and etiquette to guarantee the comfort and satisfaction of all its customers. Proper clothing is essential, with a smart casual dress code enforced in most parts of the casino. Guests are cordially advised to abstain from using mobile phones at the gaming tables and to respect the privacy and space of other guests. The casino also works under stringent age limits, having a minimum age of 18 for admittance. Proof of identity may be needed, and tourists are urged to acquaint themselves with the local gaming rules and regulations before visiting.

The Biarritz Casino is open every day, with variable hours depending on the season and day of the week. During the peak summer months, the casino normally works from 10:00 am to 4:00 am, while winter hours are often shortened to 2:00 pm to 2:00 am. It's vital to check the casino's official website or speak with your hotel concierge for the most up-to-date information on opening hours. The Biarritz Casino is readily accessible, with adequate parking available nearby. The casino is also well-connected to the town's public transit network, making it easier for guests to organize their vacations and explore the surrounding region.

A visit to the Biarritz Casino is an engaging experience that extends well beyond the gaming tables. Prepare to be charmed by the majesty of the building, the beauty of the interiors, and the bright energy that permeates the air. Wander through the sumptuous halls, enjoy the beautiful mosaics and paintings, and marvel at the breathtaking views of the Atlantic Ocean from the terrace.

Beyond the gaming floors, the casino also has a range of stores and boutiques, allowing tourists the chance to indulge in some retail therapy or explore distinctive Basque-inspired souvenirs. The on-site restaurants and bars offer the ideal backdrop for a leisurely dinner or refreshing beverage, enabling you to take in the bustling ambiance and people-watch to your heart's delight.

THE MUSÉE DE LA MER

Established in 1932, the Musée de la Mer has a strong history of maintaining and promoting the region's deep-rooted relationship to the water. Originally designed as a tiny aquarium, the museum has now expanded into a full institution that honors the rich marine life, maritime history, and oceanographic research of the Basque Country.

The museum's spectacular modernist facade, built by famous architect Louis-Marie Charpentier, quickly sets the tone for the immersive experience that awaits visitors. With its sleek, geometric lines and panoramic windows facing the Atlantic Ocean, the structure itself is a piece of art, harmoniously integrating with the spectacular natural surroundings.

As you come through the museum's doors, you'll be greeted with a stunning assortment of permanent and temporary exhibits, each painstakingly organized to engage and educate. The museum's permanent collection takes visitors on a mesmerizing voyage through the undersea world, presenting a vast diversity of marine species, from vivid coral reefs to intriguing deep-sea monsters. Interactive displays and educational exhibits give a hands-on learning experience, enabling visitors to dive deeper into the intricate ecosystems and the critical role they play in our planet's fragile balance.

In addition to the permanent galleries, the Musée de la Mer frequently offers temporary exhibits that dive into certain elements of marine science, history, and culture. These changing exhibitions typically incorporate cutting-edge research, gorgeous photography, and thought-provoking multimedia projects, ensuring that each visit to the museum is a new and fascinating experience.

One of the museum's most popular attractions is its state-of-the-art aquarium, with large tanks filled with a rich assortment of aquatic life. Visitors may marvel at the elegant motions of schools of fish, the engaging antics of playful seals, and the hypnotic light of bioluminescent species. The on-site seal sanctuary is especially significant since it offers a safe refuge for seals rescued from the Basque Coast.

Visitors may view these iconic marine animals up close, learning about the issues they face and the conservation initiatives aimed at saving them. Beyond the stunning exhibitions, the Musée de la Mer is a center of educational and interactive activities. From guided tours and seminars to hands-on activities and family-friendly events, the museum caters to visitors of all ages and interests.

Budding marine biologists may engage in specialized programs that dive into the newest scientific research, while creative minds can explore the artistic expressions inspired by the water. The museum also provides instructional tools for instructors, making it an excellent resource for schools and educational institutions in the area. To protect the comfort and safety of all visitors, the Musée de la Mer maintains a set of visiting norms and restrictions. Proper dress is essential, and guests are encouraged to avoid bringing food and drinks inside the exhibition halls.

Photography is typically allowed, except in some sensitive situations. The museum is accessible to people with impairments, and guided tours in several languages are offered upon request.

Operating hours vary by season, with the museum normally open from 10:00 am to 6:00 pm, however, it's advised to check the official website or contact the museum for the most up-to-date information. Whether you're a marine enthusiast, an inquisitive visitor, or just seeking a unique cultural experience, the Musée de la Mer in Biarritz guarantees to fascinate and inspire.

THE COTE DES BASQUES

The Côte des Basques in Biarritz, France, stands as a real jewel for those seeking a memorable beach experience. As one of the most renowned and adored sites in the area, this scenic length of coastline provides a broad assortment of activities, spectacular natural beauty, and a rich cultural past that will fascinate visitors of all ages and interests. Stretching along the rough Atlantic coastline, the Côte des Basques is a monument to the region's natural and cultural past.

Formed by the incessant hammering of the ocean, the majestic cliffs, rocky outcrops, and vast sandy beaches stand as a tribute to the strength and grandeur of the sea. The Côte des Basques has long been a hotspot of Basque culture, with a deep-rooted relationship to the water that has affected the customs, architecture, and way of life of the local people. This rich legacy is visible in the small fishing towns, the ancient structures, and the colorful festivals that dot the coastline, allowing tourists a peek into the distinctive personality of the Basque Country.

The Côte des Basques is a genuine paradise for outdoor lovers, providing a broad choice of activities and experiences for tourists to enjoy. From the famed surf breaks that pull in wave riders from across the globe to the gorgeous hiking paths that run along the clifftops, there is something to capture every adventurous soul. Surfers come to the Côte des Basques since it is home to some of the greatest and most consistent surf areas in Europe. Whether you're a seasoned pro or a newbie seeking instruction, the broad variety of waves and the thriving surf culture make this a must-visit location for wave chasers. For those wanting a more leisurely pace, the Côte des Basques also provides many chances for swimming, sunbathing, and beachcombing. The broad sandy beaches and protected coves offer the ideal environment for a calm day by the sea, with the additional pleasure of spectacular panoramic views of the Atlantic Ocean.

Beyond the beaches, the Côte des Basques features a network of scenic hiking paths that give stunning perspective points and an opportunity to immerse yourself in the region's natural magnificence. From the majestic cliffs of the Pointe Saint-Martin to the tranquil Lac Marion, these paths are a paradise for nature lovers, allowing the opportunity to discover local species, explore secret coves, and watch the ever-changing moods of the Atlantic.

At the center of the Côte des Basques is the renowned Rocher de la Vierge, a rocky outcrop connected to the mainland by a pedestrian bridge. This historic landmark provides tourists with a unique viewpoint, with panoramic views that span over the shoreline and out to the horizon. Whether you prefer to explore the region on foot or just observe the breathtaking view from the bridge, the Rocher de la Vierge is surely one of the Côte des Basques' must-see sights. The Côte des Basques is well-equipped to respond to the requirements of all guests, with a variety of services and amenities accessible along the coastline. From seaside cafés and restaurants serving up wonderful Basque cuisine to surf shops and equipment rentals, the region provides everything you need to make the most of your time by the sea. Lifeguards are stationed at the principal beaches during the peak summer months, assuring the safety and comfort of swimmers and beachgoers. Public bathrooms, showers, and change facilities are also accessible, making it simple to move from the sand to your next activity.

The Côte des Basques is readily accessible, with adequate parking available near the major beach access spots. The neighborhood is well-connected to Biarritz's public transit network, making it simple for guests to come and enjoy the coastline without the need for a private car. The Côte des Basques is open year-round, while the peak season is during the summer months when the weather is hottest and the waves are most welcoming. The beaches and hiking trails are available from sunrise till nightfall, however, it's necessary to verify local tidal schedules and any seasonal restrictions that may be in force.

THE BIARRITZ AQUARIUM

The Biarritz Aquarium stands as a real jewel for tourists seeking an immersive and awe-inspiring contact with the many marvels of the aquatic world. As one of the region's major attractions, this state-of-the-art facility allows tourists an opportunity to explore the depths of the ocean, marvel at the astonishing variety of aquatic life, and get a greater respect for the delicate ecosystems that maintain our world.

The Biarritz Aquarium has a long history going back to 1933 when it first opened its doors to the public. Over the decades, the aquarium has undergone substantial additions and modifications, growing into the spectacular institution it is today. The present structure, created by famous architect Louis-Marie Charpentier, is a masterwork of modern architecture, flawlessly merging sleek, contemporary lines with the stunning natural surroundings of the Atlantic coastline. As visitors approach the aquarium, they are instantly drawn by the spectacular glass façade, which gives a tantalizing view into the bright aquatic ecosystems that lie inside. The building's unique setting, tucked between the ocean and the scenic Biarritz promenade, further increases the sensation of immersion and connection to the marine environment.

Step through the doors of the Biarritz Aquarium, and you'll be transported into a world of captivating aquatic life, where every corner offers a discovery. The museum's skillfully selected displays feature a varied variety of marine organisms, from the bright coral reefs of the tropics to the cryptic creatures of the deep sea.

One of the aquarium's centerpieces is the big central tank, home to a dazzling assortment of sharks, rays, and other pelagic predators. Visitors may see these beautiful creatures as they glide smoothly across the water, getting greater respect for the strength and majesty of these apex predators. Beyond the main exhibition area, the Biarritz Aquarium has a range of specialty exhibits, each meant to highlight a specific facet of marine life. Discover the intriguing world of seahorses, marvel at the delicate beauty of jellyfish, and learn about the value of mangrove ecosystems and their residents. Interactive displays and touch tanks let visitors get up close and personal with chosen species, forging a closer connection with the ocean's residents.

The Biarritz Aquarium is not simply a site of wonder and amusement; it is also a center of education and conservation. The facility's committed staff of professionals' curates a full schedule of educational programs, seminars, and guided tours, appealing to visitors of all ages and interests. From interactive lectures on the value of marine biodiversity to hands-on activities that educate youngsters about the delicate balance of ocean ecosystems, the aquarium's educational efforts strive to inspire the next generation of ocean stewards. Visitors may also learn about the aquarium's continuing conservation activities, which include research, rehabilitation, and advocacy programs that strive to maintain vulnerable marine ecosystems.

The Biarritz Aquarium is open year-round, with seasonal changes in operation hours. During the peak summer months, the aquarium regularly welcomes visitors from 10:00 am to 7:00 pm, while winter hours are often limited to 10:00 am to 6:00 pm. It's best to visit the official website or consult with your hotel concierge for the most up-to-date information. The aquarium is readily accessible, with adequate parking available in the surrounding region. Visitors are welcome to bring their food and drinks, which may be eaten in the designated picnic spots. Photography is normally allowed; however, flash photography may be limited in certain sensitive exhibit locations.

Whether you're a marine lover, an inquisitive visitor, or a family seeking an instructive and amusing day out, the Biarritz Aquarium aims to fascinate and inspire. Prepare to be taken to the depths of the ocean, to wonder at the astonishing variety of aquatic life, and to depart with a deeper respect for the necessity of safeguarding our treasured marine habitats.

CHAPTER 6

OUTDOOR ADVENTURES

SURFING AND WATER SPORTS IN BIARRITZ

The lovely town of Biarritz has long been connected with the exhilarating world of surfing and water sports. As a leading location for wave riders and aquatic lovers, Biarritz provides a genuinely exceptional experience, where the strength of the Atlantic Ocean meets a rich cultural past and a dynamic coastal town. Biarritz's love affair with surfing can be traced back to the early 20th century when pioneering wave riders first discovered the region's excellent surf breaks. Over the decades, this coastal town has developed into a worldwide center for the sport, drawing surfers from across the globe who come to test their talents against the strong waves that wash over the Basque coastline.

At the heart of Biarritz's surfing culture sits the famed Côte des Basques, a stretch of coastline known for its constant and varied wave patterns. From the famed Grand Plage, with its renowned beach breakers, to the more challenging surf locations around the Uhabia and Milady beaches, Biarritz provides an abundance of possibilities to accommodate surfers of all ability levels.

The local surf community in Biarritz is dynamic and inviting, with a rich past that is strongly entwined with the region's Basque character. Surf stores, courses, and equipment rentals dot the promenades, catering to both seasoned wave riders and beginners eager to master the skill of riding the waves. While surfing may be a major attraction, Biarritz's seaside attractiveness stretches well beyond the crashing waves. The town is a true paradise for a varied spectrum of water sports lovers, giving infinite opportunities to explore the aquatic environment and push the limits of adventure.

Bodyboarding, stand-up paddle boarding (SUP), and sea kayaking are just a few of the popular water activities that flourish in Biarritz. The hidden coves and charming inlets along the coastline offer the ideal environment for these activities, enabling tourists to immerse themselves in the peacefulness of the water while taking in the breathtaking landscape. For the bravest travelers, Biarritz also has great conditions for kitesurfing and windsurfing, with the high Atlantic winds and the broad sandy beaches offering the best testing ground for these exciting sports. Beyond the ocean, the town's closeness to the Pyrenees mountains and the

Basque Country's diverse topography gives further chances for outdoor enthusiasts. Hikers, mountain bikers, and rock climbers may explore the rough terrain, further strengthening the region's attractiveness as a renowned adventure destination.

Biarritz has methodically created the infrastructure and facilities to support its booming water sports culture. Well-equipped surf schools, equipment rental businesses, and designated launch and landing places guarantee that both rookie and expert participants may enjoy their chosen sports with ease and safety. The town's beachside promenades are lined with surf-themed cafés, restaurants, and stores, providing a dynamic and friendly scene for water sports aficionados. Secure storage facilities, changing rooms, and well-maintained public utilities provide to the demands of tourists, making Biarritz a user-friendly place for aquatic excursions. Biarritz's water sports scene is impacted by the ebb and flow of the Atlantic Ocean, with seasonal fluctuations in wave conditions, wind patterns, and water temperatures. The peak surfing season normally spans from late spring to early autumn, when the waves are at their most regular and the weather is often good.

During the summer months, the town offers a range of interesting water sports events and contests, drawing top athletes and fans from across the globe. From the famed Biarritz Surf Festival to the yearly Stand-Up Paddle World Cup, these high-energy events provide visitors the opportunity to experience the peak of aquatic athletics and immerse themselves in the colorful coastal culture.

HIKING AND EXPLORING THE STUNNING COASTLINE

The coastline of Biarritz is distinguished by its towering cliffs, carved by the constant hammering of the Atlantic Ocean. These towering promontories give a vantage point for hikers to imbibe in the sweeping panoramic vistas, highlighting the rough beauty of the Basque environment. As you climb the twisting pathways, the horizon opens up, presenting a patchwork of turquoise oceans, gorgeous beaches, and attractive fishing communities that dot the coastline.

One of the most renowned coastal treks in Biarritz is the Sentier du Littoral, a well-marked and maintained route that follows the clifftops, allowing hikers a front-row seat to the strength and grandeur of the sea. Along the route, you'll find stunning coves, secret rock formations, and a rich assortment of flora and wildlife that flourish in this unique coastal environment. Interspersed throughout the hiking paths are a plethora of historic monuments and architectural jewels that give a riveting peek into Biarritz's rich cultural legacy. The Rocher de la Vierge, a beautiful rocky outcrop linked to the mainland by a charming pedestrian bridge, is a must-visit site, giving breathtaking views of the coast and the characteristic Basque architecture that borders the beach.

Another noteworthy feature is the Phare de Biarritz, a historic lighthouse that has directed seafarers for over a century. Hikers may explore the grounds of the lighthouse, learn about its legendary history, and enjoy magnificent panoramas that spread out into the beautiful seas of the Atlantic. As you traverse the meandering pathways, you'll be rewarded with the discovery of hidden coves and quiet beaches that give a tranquil escape from the more visited locations. These tucked-away jewels, accessible only by foot, give a feeling of isolation and an opportunity to interact with the natural rhythms of the shore.

One such example is the Plage de la Côte des Basques, a magnificent length of beach that is generally recognized as one of the greatest surf places in the area. Hikers may descend the cliffs to this renowned beach, where they can watch the expert surfers cut the waves, soak up the sun, or just savor the calm of the surroundings.

The seaside hiking paths of Biarritz are a refuge for nature aficionados, as they highlight a wide variety of flora and fauna that flourish in the peculiar microclimate of the Basque Country. From the brilliant wildflowers that blanket the cliff sides to the secretive sea birds that fly above, the region's abundant biodiversity is a tribute to the delicate balance of this coastal environment. Keen-eyed hikers may see the delicate motions of the local fauna, such as the playful seals that lounge on the rocky outcrops or the magnificent birds of prey that circle above. The trails also allow learning about the region's distinctive plant life, with informative signs and educational tools available along the route. The seaside hiking routes in Biarritz are well-marked and maintained, making them accessible to hikers of all ability levels. It's crucial to wear good footwear, take enough water and food, and be prepared for the varied weather conditions that might occur along the shore. Many of the trails are available year-round, while the peak season is during the summer months when the weather is most suitable. It's essential to verify local weather predictions and tidal schedules before going on your trip, since particular sections may be subject to temporary restrictions or limited access.

CYCLING AND DISCOVERING THE SURROUNDING COUNTRYSIDE

The Biarritz area is a real cyclist's paradise, with a large assortment of riding routes catering to a wide range of skill levels and interests. From calm coastal trails that hug the craggy cliffs and scenic beaches to tough hill climbs that give panoramic panoramas of the Atlantic Ocean, there's something to fascinate every style of rider. One of the most popular riding routes is the Véloroute du Littoral, a designated cycle path that travels along the coastline, affording stunning views of the crashing waves and the dramatic Basque architecture. This route is great for anyone wanting a leisurely, scenic ride, with ample chances to stop and observe the lovely coastal villages, tiny fishing ports, and ancient sites that dot the countryside. For the most ambitious riders, the undulating hills and lush, green valley's inland give a tough but rewarding trip. Tackle the meandering roads that lead to the lovely towns of Arcangues, Bidart, and Guéthary, each with its distinct character and cultural riches to explore. Along the trip, you'll be treated to breathtaking panoramas of the Pyrenees mountain range, which provide a lovely background to the Basque Country's rural splendor.

Cycling through the Biarritz countryside not only enables you to immerse yourself in the region's natural grandeur but also gives you a unique chance to dig into the lively Basque culture and culinary traditions. Stop in the picturesque village squares, where you can mix with the residents, taste handcrafted goods, and learn about the age-old rituals that have characterized this captivating corner of France. One of the must-visit sites for foodies is the town of Itxassou, noted for its extraordinary production of Ossau-Iraty, a coveted Basque sheep's milk cheese. Cycle across the rolling hills and beautiful meadows of the Nive Valley, then stop at a local fromagerie to relish in the rich, nutty tastes of this regional delicacy, accompanied by a glass of local Irouléguy wine. Beyond the gastronomic pleasures, the Biarritz landscape is filled with old churches, historical castles, and traditional Basque architecture that give a view into the region's fabled history. Stop to explore the picturesque town squares, meander through the small, winding alleyways, and connect with the friendly inhabitants, who are always happy to offer their ideas and tales.

Exploring the Biarritz countryside by bicycle is made simple, owing to the various bike rental businesses and guided tour alternatives available across the area. Many of the local hotels, tourist information centers, and specialist cycling outfitters provide high-quality bike rentals, complete with helmets, locks, and maps to assist you navigate the network of cycling paths.

For those preferring a more supervised experience, various tour companies in Biarritz offer scheduled cycling trips that appeal to a variety of skill levels and interests. These guided trips not only give the required equipment and assistance but also provide a wealth of local knowledge, enabling you to dig deeper into the history, culture, and hidden jewels of the Basque countryside.

GOLF COURSES

Biarritz's love affair with golf can be traced back to the late 19th century when the sport initially acquired popularity among the aristocratic tourists lured to the town's magnificent coastal resorts. In 1888, the Biarritz Golf Club was created, establishing one of the oldest golf clubs in continental Europe and laying the groundwork for the region's continuing status as a great golfing destination.

Over the decades, Biarritz has hosted several renowned competitions, including the French Open and the Ryder Cup, solidifying its standing as a world-class golfing center. The town's courses have been developed and improved by some of the most recognized architects in the game, each layout flawlessly integrating with the spectacular natural terrain and giving a distinct set of challenges and rewards. Biarritz features an incredible selection of golf courses, each with its unique character and delivering a distinctive playing experience. Here are a handful of the must-play sites for golf enthusiasts:

1. Biarritz Le Phare: Widely regarded as the crown gem of Biarritz's golfing scene, this classic course is recognized for its magnificent coastline backdrop and demanding links-style layout. Designed by famous architect Harry Colt, the course has dramatic elevation changes, hazardous bunkers, and breathtaking views of the Atlantic Ocean, making it a genuine test of skill and strategy.

2. Biarritz La Négresse: Nestled close inland from the ocean, this ancient course was created in 1888 and has since undergone multiple modifications, while it still has the beauty and character of its early years. Featuring tree-lined fairways, undulating greens, and a wonderful mix of par 3s, 4s, and 5s, La Négresse is a must-play for anyone wanting a classic golfing experience.

3. Biarritz Milady: Tucked away amid the Basque region, Biarritz Milady provides a tranquil and gorgeous golfing experience. Designed by famous architect Tom Simpson, the course meanders through a beautiful, parkland environment, giving players a range of difficulties, from flowing streams and strategically placed bunkers to breathtaking views of the surrounding hills.

4. Biarritz le Phare Executive Course: For those wanting a more leisurely golfing experience or wishing to warm up before tackling the region's championship-caliber layouts, the Biarritz le Phare Executive Course presents a wonderful option. This nine-hole course, located against the background of the historic Rocher de la Vierge, provides a gorgeous and entertaining game for golfers of all abilities.

Biarritz's golf courses are complemented with a multitude of superb facilities and amenities, ensuring that visitors enjoy a truly full golfing experience. Each course has well-appointed clubhouses, full pro shops, and skilled personnel to help with anything from equipment rental to lesson reservations. The area also provides a broad selection of lodgings, from quaint boutique hotels to luxurious resorts, many of which cater exclusively to the demands of golfers. Guests may enjoy on-site practice facilities, including driving ranges and putting greens, as well as access to a variety of non-golfing activities, such as spa treatments, gourmet dining, and cultural excursions.

Biarritz's golf courses are reasonably accessible, with abundant parking available at each facility. The town is well-connected to the greater transportation network, making it simple for tourists to come by car, rail, or even private aircraft. Tee times may be scheduled in advance via the individual course websites or by calling the local tourist office. It's advisable to book early, particularly during the peak summer months and popular tournament seasons, to ensure your best tee times and prevent disappointment.

Whether you're a seasoned golfer or a beginner to the sport, Biarritz's superb golf offers a guarantee to give a wonderful experience. From the spectacular coastline layouts to the calm interior courses, the region's golfing options effortlessly integrate natural beauty, historic legacy, and world-class services, making it a must-visit destination for every discriminating golf fan.

CASINO BARRIÈRE

The Casino Barrière of Biarritz shines as a beacon of glamor, entertainment, and cultural diversity. As one of the most recognizable and compelling attractions in the area, this renowned gaming and entertainment complex gives tourists a comprehensive experience that goes well beyond the usual casino experience. The Casino Barrière's stunning neoclassical-style architecture, with its big façade and decorative decorations, quickly sets the tone for the luxurious and elegant ambiance that pervades the whole complex. Constructed in the late 19th century, the casino's architectural legacy is a testimony to the town's famous past as a leading European tourist destination.

As you pass through the majestic entryway, you'll be taken back in time, with the sumptuous décor and painstaking attention to detail reflecting the grandeur of a bygone period. The magnificent chandeliers, the complex moldings, and the dazzling marble floors all add to the casino's irresistible attractiveness and feeling of grandeur.

At the core of the Casino Barrière's lies its world-class gaming facilities, serving both seasoned high rollers and casual gamers alike. From the thrill of roulette and blackjack to the compelling draw of slot machines, the casino's gaming floors are alive with the excitement of chance and the quest of Lady Luck. The casino's staff of professional croupiers and dealers ensures that every contact is defined by great service and attention to detail, ensuring a flawless and delightful gaming experience for all its visitors. Whether you want to test your abilities at the tables or just take in the bustling ambiance, the Casino Barrière delivers an outstanding gaming experience.

Beyond the gaming tables, the Casino Barrière is a genuine gastronomic destination, providing a broad assortment of eating choices that appeal to every flavor and inclination. From the beautiful and refined restaurant, with its outstanding French and Basque-inspired food, to the more informal and vibrant bistros and pubs, the casino's gastronomic offerings are a great highlight for guests. Savor the rich tastes of local dishes, indulge in inventive and masterfully made drinks, and immerse yourself in the bustling environment that pervades the casino's eating locations. Whether you're seeking a romantic evening or a raucous gathering with friends, the Casino Barrière's gastronomic offerings are guaranteed to make a memorable impression.

The Casino Barrière's dedication to entertainment goes well beyond the gaming tables, with a busy program of events, performances, and cultural activities that appeal to a broad variety of interests. From live music and cabaret acts to art exhibits and cultural festivals, the casino's event rooms deliver a vibrant and ever-changing array of events. Witness the fascinating talent of famous musicians, comedians, and dancers, or discover the rich cultural legacy of the Basque area via immersive exhibits and interactive workshops. The casino's event schedule is a real representation of the eclectic and cosmopolitan culture of Biarritz, allowing guests a chance to enjoy the town's distinctive combination of French and Basque influences.

The Casino Barrière is open year-round, with different hours of operation depending on the season and day of the week. During the peak summer months, the casino regularly welcomes customers from 10:00 am to 4:00 am, while winter hours are often limited to 2:00 pm to 2:00 am. It's vital to check the casino's official website or chat with your hotel concierge for the most up-to-date information on opening hours. The casino is readily accessible, with adequate parking available in the surrounding region. The facility is also well-connected to Biarritz's public transit network, making it simple for guests to organize their vacations and explore the greater area.

Visitors are respectfully requested to conform to the casino's dress code, which normally demands smart casual clothes. Additionally, the minimum age for access is 18 years old, and visitors may be requested to produce proper identification upon entrance.

Whether you're a seasoned gambler, a fan of live entertainment, or just seeking a unique cultural experience, the Casino Barrière in Biarritz aims to captivate and please. Prepare to be carried away by the grandeur, the excitement, and the ageless attraction of this famous institution, which stands as a tribute to the lasting attractiveness of Biarritz as a prime destination for tourists from across the globe.

CHAPTER 7

DAY TRIPS FROM BIARRITZ

SAN SEBASTIÁN, SPAIN

For visitors visiting the gorgeous coastal resort of Biarritz, France, a day excursion to the charming city of San Sebastián, Spain, is a must-add to the itinerary. Nestled just over the border, a short 30 minutes from Biarritz, San Sebastián offers a plethora of cultural, gastronomic, and natural delights that are guaranteed to fascinate and thrill.

Reaching San Sebastián from Biarritz is a snap, with a range of simple transit alternatives available. The most direct method is via automobile, with the trip lasting roughly 30 minutes along the picturesque A-8 highway. Alternatively, travelers may choose for the bus, with frequent trips linking the two cities throughout the day.

For a more leisurely experience, the train is another wonderful alternative, with the ride lasting roughly 45 minutes and affording panoramic views of the lovely Basque landscape. Regardless of the form of transportation, the journey is incredibly quick and uncomplicated, making San Sebastián a perfect day trip destination for guests residing in Biarritz.

Upon arriving in San Sebastián, the first destination for many tourists is the city's charming Old Town, a maze of cobblestone alleyways and medieval buildings that emanates Basque charm. Wander around the colorful plazas, see the stunning 16th-century Basilica of Santa María, and immerse yourself in the vibrant ambiance of the local markets and artisan stores.

One of the attractions of the Old Town is the famed Concha Bay, a crescent-shaped length of sand that is regarded as one of the most beautiful urban beaches in Europe. Take a leisurely walk down the promenade, stop for a refreshing pintxo (Basque-style tapas) at one of the numerous bars, and enjoy the spectacular views of the surrounding hills and the Isla de Santa Clara.

San Sebastián is recognized for its extraordinary gastronomic scene, earning it the distinguished title of the "Food Capital of Europe." As a day tripper, you'll be spoilt for choice when it comes to partaking in the city's culinary pleasures. Begin your gastronomic tour by immersing yourself in the bustling pintxo culture, bouncing from bar to bar, and enjoying the varied assortment of tiny, expertly made snacks. For a more elevated dining experience, head to one of the city's world-renowned Michelin-starred restaurants, where you can sample inventive meals that highlight the best local ingredients and the extraordinary abilities of the region's top chefs. Beyond the famed restaurants, San Sebastián is also home to a thriving food market, the Mercado de la Bretxa, where you can peruse the stalls, engage with local producers, and buy high-quality Basque dishes to savor during your day.

While San Sebastián is recognized for its gastronomic and cultural attractions, the city also provides a multitude of outdoor adventures and magnificent natural landscapes. Take a leisurely trek up Mount Igueldo, where you'll be rewarded with magnificent views of the city, the Cantabrian Sea, and the neighboring Basque hills.

Alternatively, discover the rough coastline and secret bays by following the magnificent route that weaves its way along the cliffs. For a unique viewpoint, try riding the funicular train to the summit of Mount Igueldo, where you can experience exciting amusement park rides and observe the breathtaking panoramas from the old lighthouse and observation deck. Beyond the gastronomic and environmental beauties, San Sebastián is also a center of cultural variety and creative expression. Visit the San Telmo Museoa, a famous institution that highlights the rich history and customs of the Basque Country, or explore the modern art galleries and museums that dot the city's colorful districts. Attend a play at the exquisite Victoria Eugenia Theatre, marvel at the magnificent Belle Époque architecture, or join the residents in enjoying one of the numerous festivals and events that take place throughout the year, such as the famous San Sebastián International Film Festival.

BAYONNE AND ANGLET

For tourists visiting the coastal resort of Biarritz, France, a day excursion to the adjacent towns of Bayonne and Anglet provides a multitude of cultural, historical, and natural activities that are guaranteed to improve your Basque Country vacation. Situated only a short distance from Biarritz, these two bustling places offer a wonderful complement to your stay, enabling you to dig further into the region's rich legacy and different landscapes.

The travel from Biarritz to Bayonne and Anglet is a smooth and easy one, with a multitude of transportation alternatives available. By automobile, the distance between the three cities is around 15 kilometers (9 miles), and the travel takes around 20-25 minutes, depending on traffic.

Alternatively, you may choose the local bus service, which runs frequently between the towns and takes around 30 minutes. For those preferring a more leisurely means of transit, the Basque Coast Train (Abarka) links Biarritz, Bayonne, and Anglet, providing a lovely and pleasant ride along the gorgeous coastline. The entire trip time by rail is roughly 15-20 minutes, making it possible to see all three attractions in a single day.

Situated at the junction of the Nive and Adour rivers, the ancient city of Bayonne is famed for its well-preserved medieval architecture, rich cultural legacy, and exquisite gastronomic pleasures. As you arrive in Bayonne, you'll be instantly charmed by the lovely old town, with its small winding lanes, half-timbered buildings, and attractive market squares. Begin your trip with the majestic Bayonne Cathedral, a beautiful Gothic monument that exemplifies the region's Basque-influenced architectural style. Wander around the neighboring Remparts (city walls) and Citadel, which give panoramic views of the surrounding metropolis and the river below. History aficionados will also be attracted by the Musée Basque, a fascinating museum that digs into the rich cultural traditions and practices of the Basque people.

No visit to Bayonne is complete without partaking in the city's famed gastronomic delicacies. Sample the legendary Bayonne ham, a delicacy that has been cured and matured to perfection, or relish the traditional Basque pintxos (the Basque equivalent of tapas) in the vibrant city center.

Just a short distance from Bayonne, the seaside town of Anglet provides a stunning combination of natural beauty and outdoor leisure. As you arrive at Anglet, you'll be met with the spectacular Côte des Basques, a length of pure sandy beaches and towering cliffs that have long been a paradise for surfers and beach aficionados. Spend some time wandering along the beachside promenade, soaking in the spectacular views of the Atlantic Ocean and the rolling Basque hills in the background.

For the adventurous, Anglet is a fantastic location for surfing, with numerous famous surf areas that cater to all ability levels. If you're not a surfer, try hiring a bike and exploring the town's enormous network of bicycle trails, which run through stunning coastal vistas and pleasant neighborhoods. Beyond the beaches, Anglet is also home to the Abbadie Castle, a spectacular 19th-century manor house that today houses a museum devoted to the region's history and culture. The castle's grounds and adjoining parklands offer a serene refuge for a leisurely walk or a picnic. To make the most of your day travel from Biarritz to Bayonne and Anglet, consider the following itinerary:

Morning: Start your day in Bayonne, touring the ancient old town, the Bayonne Cathedral, and the Musée Basque. Indulge in a typical Basque breakfast or brunch, appreciating the local delights.

Afternoon: Travel to Anglet and spend time along the magnificent Côte des Basques, either sunbathing on the beach, surfing, or cycling along the coastal pathways. Visit Abbadie Castle and walk around the calm grounds.

Evening: Return to Bayonne and immerse yourself in the busy city center, tasting the native pintxos and possibly a bottle of Basque wine.

This itinerary enables you to explore the rich history, lively culture, and spectacular natural beauty that distinguish the Bayonne-Anglet area, complimenting your visit to the lovely town of Biarritz.

PYRENEES MOUNTAINS

The Pyrenees Mountains are located around 100 kilometers (62 miles) from Biarritz, making it a readily accessible day trip destination. Depending on your means of transportation and the precise route selected, the travel can normally be accomplished in roughly 1.5 to 2 hours each way, allowing you adequate time to explore the area. For your day excursion to the Pyrenees from Biarritz, there are various suitable options:

Rental vehicle: Renting a vehicle provides the utmost freedom and liberty to explore the Pyrenees at your speed. This is a fantastic option if you wish to stop at numerous overlooks, hiking trails, or tiny communities along the road.

Private transport: You may arrange for a private transport service, which will pick you up from your lodgings in Biarritz and take you straight to the Pyrenees. This option is suitable for individuals who desire a more relaxed and hassle-free experience.

Public transit: If you choose not to drive, you may take a bus or train from Biarritz to the next town or city in the Pyrenees, such as Pau or Lourdes, and then utilize local transit or guided excursions to explore the area.

The Pyrenees Mountains run around 430 kilometers (270 miles) along the border between France and Spain, with the tallest peaks reaching over 3,000 meters (9,800 feet) in height. As a day excursion from Biarritz, you might concentrate on the French side of the Pyrenees, which provides a broad selection of scenery and attractions. Some of the must-see highlights in the Pyrenees include:

1. Pic du Midi de Bigorre: This prominent mountain summit provides panoramic views of the Pyrenees and is accessible via cable car. Visitors may enjoy spectacular panoramas, tour the observatory, and learn about the region's history and geology.

2. **Cirque de Gavarnie:** A UNESCO World Heritage Site, the Cirque de Gavarnie is a stunning natural amphitheater formed by glaciers, including towering cliffs and gushing waterfalls. Hiking routes allow access to beautiful vistas and the Gavarnie Falls, one of the tallest waterfalls in Europe.

3. **Lourdes:** This modest town is famed for its Roman Catholic Marian shrine, the Sanctuary of Our Lady of Lourdes, which draws millions of people each year. Visitors may visit the Basilica of the Immaculate Conception, the Grotto of Massabielle, and the surrounding holy attractions.

4. **Pyrenees National Park:** This protected natural environment provides a plethora of outdoor activities, including hiking, mountain biking, and animal watching.

Visitors may experience the park's various habitats, including alpine meadows, glacial lakes, and historic beech woods. Here's a typical one-day schedule to make the most of your Pyrenees day trip from Biarritz:

9:00 AM - Depart Biarritz and travel towards the Pyrenees, stopping at picturesque overlooks along the route.

11:00 AM - Arrive at the Pic du Midi de Bigorre and ride the cable car to the peak for panoramic views.

1:00 PM - Drive to the Cirque de Gavarnie and begin on a modest climb to the beautiful Gavarnie Falls.

3:30 PM - Visit the town of Lourdes and see the Sanctuary of Our Lady of Lourdes and its ancient religious attractions.

5:30 PM - Depart Lourdes and make your way back to Biarritz, with an optional stop at a nearby Pyrenean village or vineyard.

8:00 PM - Arrive back in Biarritz, having enjoyed the natural beauty and cultural richness of the Pyrenees Mountains.

In addition to the activities highlighted, the Pyrenees provide a multitude of activities and attractions for travelers:

- **Hiking:** Explore a huge network of hiking routes, ranging from short walks to demanding hikes, affording spectacular views of the mountains, valleys, and alpine lakes.

- **Outdoor Adventures:** Enjoy sports such as mountain biking, rock climbing, canyoning, and even ski resorts during the winter months.

- **Cultural Immersion:** Visit picturesque Pyrenean villages, eat local food and wines, and learn about the region's rich history and customs.

- **Wildlife Observation:** Keep a watch out for different animals, including the distinctive Pyrenean brown bear, chamois, and a range of bird species.

Whether you're a nature enthusiast, a cultural adventurer, or just seeking a spectacular day excursion from Biarritz, the Pyrenees Mountains provide an amazing experience. With its breathtaking views, outdoor activities, and historical importance, this day excursion is likely to make a lasting impact on any tourist.

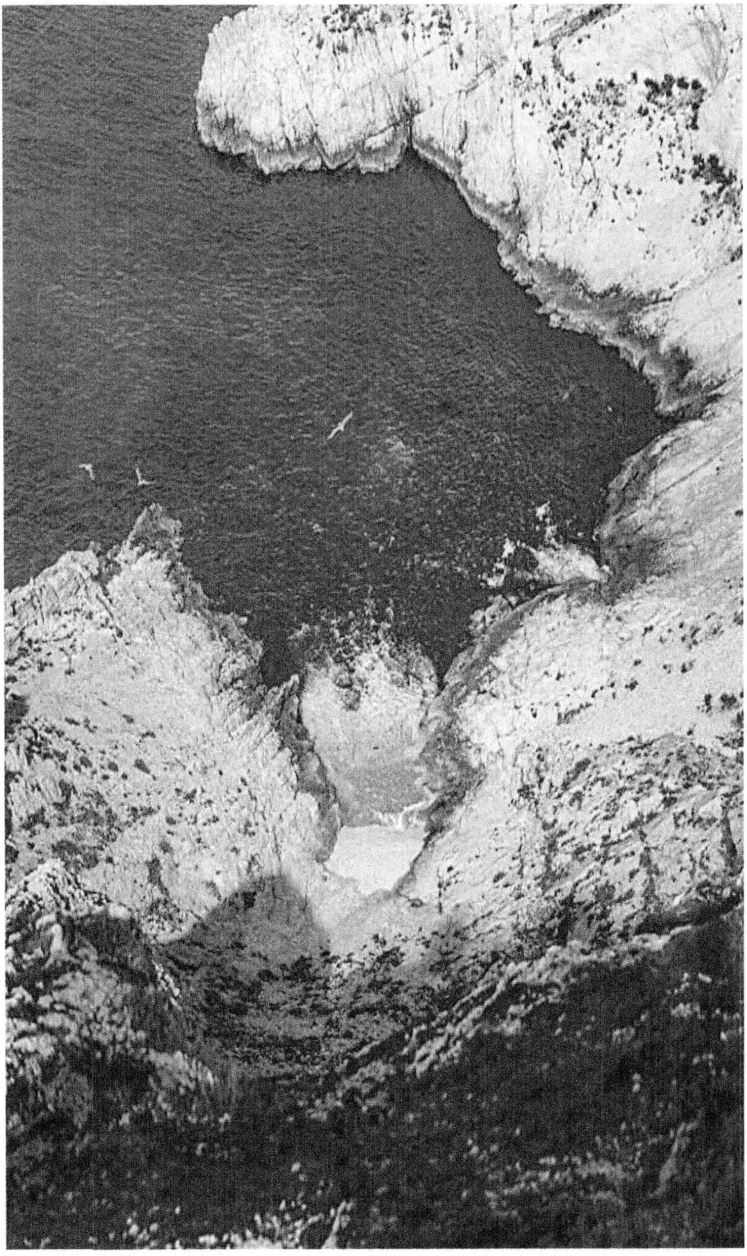

CHAPTER 8

PRACTICAL TIPS AND INFORMATION

VISA AND ENTRY REQUIREMENTS

Biarritz, located in the Nouvelle-Aquitaine area, is a popular destination for both domestic and foreign travelers, and it's crucial to grasp the required papers and procedures to guarantee a smooth and hassle-free voyage.

European Union (EU) Citizens: For tourists from inside the European Union, including nations like Germany, Spain, Italy, and the United Kingdom, no visa is necessary to enter France. EU nationals may easily enter Biarritz and the rest of France with a valid national identification card or passport. The freedom of movement inside the Schengen Area, of which France is a member, permits EU residents to visit and remain in Biarritz and other French territories without the need for a visa.

Non-European Union Citizens: Travelers from non-EU nations, such as the United States, Canada, Australia, and others, normally need a visa to enter France, including Biarritz. The particular visa requirements will depend on the traveler's nationality and the purpose and length of their trip. For travelers considering a brief journey to Biarritz, normally not exceeding 90 days, a Schengen visa is necessary. The Schengen visa is a single-entry permit that permits the bearer to travel freely throughout the Schengen Area, which includes France and most other European Union nations. To get a Schengen visa, non-EU nationals must apply to the French embassy or consulate in their place of residence, well in advance of their scheduled trip dates. The application procedure normally requires delivering the following documents:

- A completed and signed Schengen visa application form.
- A valid passport or travel document with at least two blank pages.
- Proof of trip plans, such as airline itineraries, hotel bookings, or a letter of invitation.
- Evidence of adequate financial resources to support the expense of the trip, such as bank statements or a letter from the employer.
- Travel health insurance with a minimum coverage of €30,000 for medical bills and repatriation.
- Additional supporting papers may be necessary, depending on the purpose of the trip (e.g., proof of lodging, evidence of work, or a letter from the employer).

The processing period for a Schengen visa application might vary, so it's crucial to apply well in advance, often at least 4-6 weeks before the scheduled trip date. For tourists wishing to remain in Biarritz or France for more than 90 days, a long-stay visa or residency permit may be necessary. This group comprises persons who want to study, work, or dwell in France for a lengthy duration.

The application procedure for a long-stay visa or residence permit is more difficult and entails extra criteria, such as evidence of adequate financial means, a solid case for the longer stay, and often a medical assessment. It's essential to remember that the visa and entrance requirements for France, including Biarritz, are subject to change, and tourists should always check the latest information with the French government or the closest French embassy or consulate before arranging their trip. Regardless of your country, it's strongly encouraged to thoroughly research the visa and entrance requirements well in advance of your journey to Biarritz, France. This will enable a smooth and stress-free arrival and allow you to completely immerse yourself in the beauty and charm of this seaside jewel.

LOCAL LAWS AND CUSTOMS

Biarritz, situated in the Nouvelle-Aquitaine region of southern France, is noted for its stunning beaches, lively culture, and rich history. To make the most of your stay in Biarritz and prevent any inadvertent blunders, it's necessary to educate yourself with the following major features of local laws and traditions.

Public Conduct and Etiquette: Biarritz is a cosmopolitan and hospitable place, but it's necessary to be cognizant of local social standards and etiquette. Visitors are required to behave themselves politely and courteously, abstaining from noisy or disruptive behavior, especially in public locations and during the nighttime hours.

Dress Code & Attire: While Biarritz is a somewhat casual and laidback town, there are certain fundamental standards to remember when it comes to proper clothes. In most public venues, such as restaurants, stores, and cultural organizations, casual but tidy and clean clothes are often appropriate. However, it's preferable to dress more formally while visiting religious places or attending particular activities.

Smoking Regulations: France, particularly Biarritz, has strong rules regulating smoking in public areas. Smoking is forbidden in all interior public locations, such as restaurants, bars, and public buildings. Visitors are encouraged to only smoke in specified outside locations to avoid any fines or penalties.

Alcohol Consumption: The legal drinking age in France is 18 years old. While the drinking of alcohol is largely permitted in Biarritz, especially in social contexts, tourists should be aware of their alcohol intake and avoid public drunkenness, since this might result in penalties or even legal repercussions.

Environmental Awareness and Conservation: Biarritz is devoted to sustainable tourism and environmental conservation. Travelers are required to be careful of their influence on the local environment and to adopt eco-friendly habits, such as properly disposing of garbage, conserving water, and preserving the natural scenery.

Photographing and Filming: While photography and recording are normally allowed in public locations, visitors should be respectful and avoid upsetting people or collecting photographs without their agreement, especially in private or sensitive areas.

Public Transportation and Parking: Biarritz has a well-developed public transit infrastructure, including buses and taxis. Visitors are recommended to acquaint themselves with the local schedules and restrictions, as well as to utilize approved parking spots to prevent any penalties or towing.

Cultural Sensitivity and Respect: Biarritz has a rich cultural legacy, and tourists are encouraged to demonstrate respect and attention while interacting with local customs, traditions, and religious practices. Visitors should be cautious of acceptable conduct while visiting historic sites, houses of worship, or participating in cultural activities.

Emergency and Safety Protocols: In the case of an emergency, tourists should be informed of the local emergency numbers and follow the directions of local authorities. Additionally, it's suggested to register with your embassy or consulate and purchase comprehensive travel insurance to safeguard your safety and well-being throughout your time in Biarritz. By familiarizing themselves with these local rules and practices, tourists visiting Biarritz may ensure a courteous, enjoyable, and trouble-free trip. Remember, embracing the local culture and sticking to the laws and regulations in Biarritz will not only increase your pleasure of the trip but also contribute to the general well-being of the town.

CURRENCY AND BUDGET PLANNING

The official currency used in Biarritz, as well as across France, is the Euro (EUR or €). The Euro is the single currency shared by 19 of the 27 member nations of the European Union, including France. It's vital to be aware of the Euro's value and exchange rate relative to your local money since this will be key for making purchases and monitoring your expenditures throughout your trip.

Before going for Biarritz, it's a good idea to check the current conversion rate between your local currency and the Euro. You may discover up-to-date exchange rates online, via your bank, or by utilizing currency conversion applications. Keep in mind that exchange rates may vary, so it's good to check them leading up to and throughout your trip. When it comes to converting currencies, you have numerous options:

I. Exchanging your native currency for Euros before your trip: This may be done at your local bank, currency exchange bureaus, or even at the airport before your departure. This enables you to have Euros on hand as soon as you arrive in Biarritz, which may be useful for making early purchases and payments.

II. Withdrawing Euros from ATMs in Biarritz: Using your debit or credit card to withdraw Euros from local ATMs is generally the most cost-effective option to access cash during your vacation. Most banks and ATMs in Biarritz will take major foreign cards, and you may even obtain a better exchange rate compared to converting money at a bureau de change.

III. Using credit/debit cards for purchases: Many establishments in Biarritz, including hotels, restaurants, and stores, take major credit and debit cards, including Visa, Mastercard, and American Express. This may be a handy alternative since you won't need to carry big quantities of cash. However, it's necessary to advise your card issuer of your vacation intentions and check for any international transaction fees.

Creating a clear budget for your vacation to Biarritz is vital to guarantee you have a pleasurable and stress-free time. Consider the following criteria while preparing your budget:

I. Accommodation: Research and compare costs for hotels, vacation rentals, or hostels in Biarritz to discover the best choice that matches your budget. Consider the location, facilities, and reviews while making your pick.

II. Transportation: Factor in the price of traveling to and from Biarritz, as well as any local transportation you may require, such as taxis, buses, or trains. If you want to hire a vehicle, add the rental charge, gasoline costs, and parking fees.

III. Meals & eating: Biarritz is recognized for its superb food, so make sure to set a fair budget for dining out at restaurants, cafés, and small eateries. Don't forget to account for any snacks, beverages, or groceries you may need.

IV. Excursions and attractions: Research the pricing of any excursions, tours, or admission fees for the sites and attractions you intend to see in Biarritz. This will help you prepare correctly and prevent unforeseen costs.

V. Miscellaneous expenditures: Don't forget to add a buffer in your budget for incidental fees, such as souvenirs, gratuities, or unforeseen expenses that may develop during your trip.

By properly knowing the currency, and conversion rates, and planning for your vacation to Biarritz, France, you can assure a financially stress-free and delightful time. Remember to maintain your exchange rate information up-to-date, employ simple payment options, and manage your finances carefully to make the most of your stay in this lovely seaside resort.

SHOPPING AND SOUVENIRS

Biarritz has always been a sanctuary for the well-heeled and trendy, and this is reflected in its stunning assortment of high-end shops and luxury businesses. Stroll down the Rue Gambetta, the major shopping strip, and you'll discover the flagship boutiques of famous French and worldwide luxury brands, such as Chanel, Louis Vuitton, Hermès, and Dior. These beautiful shops display the newest collections in fashion, accessories, jewelry, and beauty goods, catering to individuals in search of rare and expensive things.

Beyond the glamor of the luxury labels, Biarritz is also home to a flourishing community of local craftsmen and crafters. Explore the lovely side alleys and laneways to uncover unique businesses providing handmade products, traditional Basque fabrics, and one-of-a-kind souvenirs. From ceramics and pottery to delicate lace and complex woodcarvings, these stores provide a look into the rich tradition and skill of the Basque area.

No vacation to Biarritz is complete without a visit to the famed Les Halles de Biarritz, the city's principal indoor market. This busy center is a great sensory feast, with kiosks brimming with fresh local vegetables, regional delicacies, and artisanal culinary products. Wander around the aisles, try the delectable cheeses, charcuterie, and freshly baked bread, and immerse yourself in the lively local culinary culture.

Les Halles is also a fantastic spot to stock up on gourmet souvenirs and presents to take back home. As you explore the numerous shopping places in Biarritz, you'll find a selection of unique and valued gifts to mark your vacation. Here are some of the top things to look for:

1. Basque Espadrilles: The traditional Basque footwear, known as espadrilles, is a typical memento from Biarritz. These comfy and elegant shoes come in a range of colors and styles, frequently sporting the signature Basque cross symbol.

2. Bayonne Ham: The famed Bayonne ham, a delicacy of the Basque area, is a must-have keepsake. Purchase whole or sliced hams, as well as other Basque charcuterie items, to appreciate the rich, savory taste of this native delicacy.

3. Basque Linen & Textiles: The Basque area is recognized for its superb linen and textile workmanship. Look for traditional Basque-style tablecloths, napkins, and other household products displaying the region's unique patterns and motifs.

4. Basque Pottery & Ceramics: Biarritz is home to various handmade pottery and ceramic studios, creating exquisite items that represent the Basque region's creative heritage. Consider acquiring beautiful plates, mugs, or sculptures to bring a bit of Basque character to your house.

5. Béret Basque: The famous Basque beret, a sign of the region's cultural history, provides for a timeless and functional keepsake. These traditional hats come in a variety of hues and may be bought at specialist stores across Biarritz.

As you immerse yourself in the shopping experience of Biarritz, remember to give adequate time to explore, discover, and delight in the unique and compelling offers of this quaint French city.

HEALTH AND SAFETY CONSIDERATIONS

France has a well-developed and efficient healthcare system that delivers excellent medical services to both inhabitants and tourists. In Biarritz, you'll discover a choice of healthcare facilities, including public and private hospitals, clinics, and pharmacies, that may cater to your medical requirements. It's crucial to realize that as a tourist, you may not be immediately covered by the French national healthcare system, known as the Sécurité Sociale. Therefore, it's vital to have sufficient travel health insurance or a European Health Insurance Card (EHIC) to guarantee you can obtain and pay the cost of any required medical care during your stay.

Before your journey, speak with your healthcare practitioner to verify you are up-to-date with any required immunizations for travel to France. Additionally, if you frequently take any prescription drugs, be sure you pack appropriate amounts and have a copy of your prescription with you. Be aware that certain prescriptions may have different names or formulas in France, so it's a good idea to study the availability and equivalents of your medications in the nation.

If you need to refill or acquire drugs during your stay, find a local pharmacy and chat with the pharmacist. Biarritz boasts a warm, oceanic environment, but you should still be prepared for the local weather conditions and seasonal fluctuations.

Biarritz's coastline position means you'll be exposed to intense light and UV rays, particularly during the summer months. Protect yourself by applying sunscreen with a high SPF, a hat, and sunglasses while spending time outdoors. Be careful of the sun's intensity, and take rests in the shade to avoid sunburn and heat-related diseases. Biarritz is famed for its magnificent beaches, but it's vital to be mindful of possible risks, like strong currents, rip tides, and occasional jellyfish or other marine life. Follow the directions and cautions given by local authorities, and only swim in specified, supervised locations.

Depending on the time of year, Biarritz may encounter varied weather conditions. During the winter months, the weather might be chilly and wet, so bring suitable clothes and be prepared for unexpected interruptions to transit or outdoor activities. In the summer, the town may get extremely congested, so prepare appropriately and be aware of your safety in major public places. Biarritz is considered a secure and low-crime location, but as with any vacation, it's vital to take reasonable care to guarantee your safety. While serious crime is uncommon, Biarritz, like many major tourist sites, may face incidences of petty crime, like French pickpocketing or bag snatching, especially in congested areas or near transit hubs. Keep your possessions secure, avoid showcasing costly stuff, and be mindful of your surroundings.

Biarritz is situated in an area that might sometimes encounter natural catastrophes, such as strong rains, floods, or infrequent wildfires. Familiarize yourself with emergency procedures and remain updated about any weather alerts or advisories throughout your stay. By being proactive and aware of the health and safety issues for Biarritz, you may have a worry-free and enjoyable trip to this picturesque seaside town in France. Remember to study, prepare, and take reasonable steps to guarantee your well-being and have a safe and great trip to Biarritz.

SAFETY TIPS AND EMERGENCY CONTACTS

1. Personal Safety: Be vigilant of your surroundings, particularly in busy settings or at night. Avoid exhibiting costly things or valuables, and keep your stuff close to you. Use cross-body bags or handbags with secure closures to avoid pickpockets. Avoid wandering alone at night and stick to well-lit, busy places. Trust your instincts and remove yourself from any situation that makes you feel uncomfortable.

2. Petty Crime Prevention: Keep your wallet, phone, and other valuables safe in an internal pocket or a money belt. Photocopy or digitally save crucial papers, such as your passport, in case of loss or theft. Be careful while using ATMs, and avoid utilizing them in secluded or poorly lighted places. Keep a tight check on your valuables whether eating, shopping, or utilizing public transit.

3. Beach and Water Safety: Familiarize yourself with the beach flags and warning systems, and only swim in specified, supervised areas. Beware of strong currents, rip tides, and other ocean risks, and heed the recommendations of lifeguards. Protect yourself from the sun by wearing sunscreen, a hat, and sunglasses. Stay hydrated and rest in the shade to minimize heat-related diseases.

4. Transportation Safety: Use official taxis or ridesharing services, and avoid unregistered or unmarked cars. When utilizing public transportation, keep your possessions close and be mindful of your surroundings. If hiring a vehicle, acquaint yourself with local traffic rules and driving norms.

5. Natural Disaster Preparedness: Familiarize yourself with emergency procedures and any weather advisories or warnings. Identify the location of your closest emergency shelter or designated safe zone. Keep your mobile device charged and have a backup power source ready.

Emergency Services:
- Emergency number (fire, police, ambulance): 112
- Police: 17
- Fire Department: 18
- Emergency Medical Services: 15

Useful Contacts:
- US Embassy in Paris: +33 1 43 12 22 22
- Canadian Embassy in Paris: +33 1 44 43 29 00
- UK Embassy in Paris: +33 1 44 51 31 00
- Australian Embassy in Paris: +33 1 40 59 33 00

Local Contacts:
- Biarritz Tourist Office: +33 5 59 22 37 00

- Biarritz Hospital (Centre Hospitalier de la Côte Basque): +33 5 59 44 40 00
- Biarritz Pharmacy (Pharmacie): +33 5 59 24 27 96

By familiarizing yourself with these safety guidelines and emergency contact information, you may go to Biarritz with confidence and peace of mind. Remember to keep vigilant, trust your instincts, and observe local norms to have a safe and pleasurable time in this lovely French seaside town.

CONCLUSION

Thank you for reading our detailed Biarritz, France travel guide! We hope that our guide has supplied you with all the essential information to organize an exciting and safe vacation to this gorgeous seaside town.

Biarritz, with its rich history, spectacular natural beauty, and active local culture, is a wonderfully intriguing location that can attract and inspire people from across the globe. From navigating the currency and exchange rates to exploring the diverse shopping and souvenir options, and from understanding the local health and safety considerations to having the necessary emergency contacts at hand, we've covered all the essential details to ensure you have a seamless and enjoyable experience.

As you begin on your trip to Biarritz, we advise you to experience the laid-back, but elegant appeal of this Basque treasure. Stroll down the promenade, enjoy the famous local cuisine, and immerse yourself in the unique combination of French and Basque traditions that make Biarritz so remarkable.

Remember, the key to a genuinely wonderful vacation is being prepared and educated. By following the suggestions and advice offered in this book, you can concentrate on creating lasting memories and making the most of your stay in the enchanting town of Biarritz. We wish you a nice and safe vacation in Biarritz, France. Bon journey!

BIDDING FAREWELL TO BIARRITZ

As your stay in the seaside town of Biarritz, France, draws to a conclusion, it's normal to experience a bittersweet combination of feelings. The stunning beauty, rich culture, and friendly hospitality of Biarritz have left an everlasting impact on your heart and mind. In this note, we'll help you reflect on your experience and give advice to ensure you leave Biarritz with a lasting appreciation for this great location.

Take a minute to reflect on the highlights of your stay in Biarritz. Perhaps it was the stunning vistas from the Rocher de la Vierge, the adrenaline of watching the crashing waves at the Grande Plage, or the delicious tastes of the native Basque cuisine that left the deepest imprints.

Recall the moments that resonated most with you and the bonds you established with the welcoming locals. Before you go, be sure you capture as many memories as possible to enjoy long after your departure. Organize your images, write a trip diary, or gather tiny trinkets that will remind you of your Biarritz experience. These physical souvenirs can allow you to recall the enchantment of this seaside jewel anytime you wish.

As you wave goodbye to Biarritz, consider methods to share your experiences with friends, family, and loved ones back home. Prepare a slideshow or a thorough presentation presenting the breathtaking landscape, cultural highlights, and personal experiences from your trip. This not only helps you to relive your vacation but also motivates others to add Biarritz to their travel bucket lists.

Take the time to express your appreciation to the persons who have contributed to the success of your Biarritz journey. This may include hotel personnel, restaurant waiters, tour guides, or any locals who have gone out of their way to make your stay more pleasurable. A few nice words or a tiny gesture of thanks may go a long way in making a favorable impression and deepening the links between tourists and the host community.

As you leave Biarritz, contemplate the prospect of a future return. This lovely village has a way of attracting tourists, and you may find yourself wishing to relive its attractions. Make a mental note of any activities, eateries, or hidden treasures you intend to explore more on your future visit. Additionally, don't hesitate to promote Biarritz to your friends, family, and other tourists. Share your views, recommendations, and experiences, motivating others to go on their own Biarritz voyage and discover the enchantment of this seaside treasure in the Basque region of France.

As you wave goodbye to Biarritz, realize that the experiences and relationships you've formed will live on, acting as a tribute to the deep influence this extraordinary place has had on your life. With a heart full of thanks and a mind bursting with beloved memories, you farewell Biarritz, knowing that a part of you will always stay in this beautiful seaside town.

SCAN THE QR CODE BELOW TO GET ACCESS TO MORE BOOKS BY THE AUTHOR

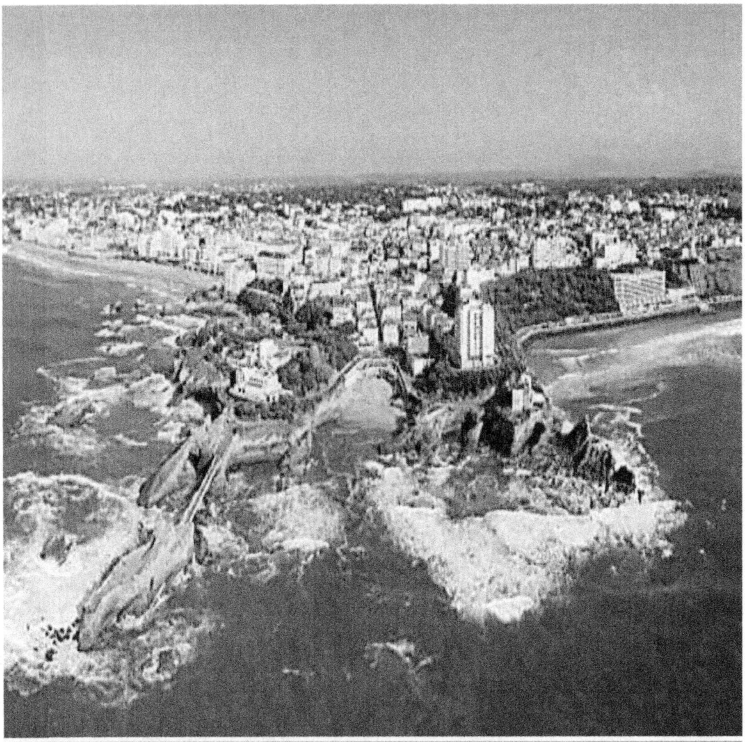

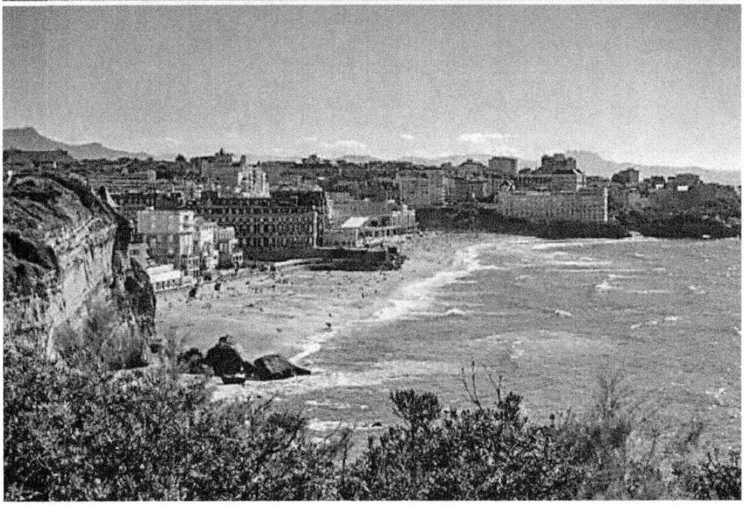

Printed in Great Britain
by Amazon